BLACKPOOL
AT WAR

BLACKPOOL AT WAR

A HISTORY OF THE FYLDE COAST DURING the SECOND WORLD WAR

JOHN ELLIS

*In memory of all those on the Fylde who made
the ultimate sacrifice during the conflict
for the freedom of future generations.*

First published 2013

The History Press
The Mill, Brimscombe Port
Stroud, Gloucestershire, GL5 2QG
www.thehistorypress.co.uk

British Library Cataloguing in Publication Data.
A catalogue record for this book is available from the British Library.

ISBN 978 0 7524 8583 6

Typesetting and origination by The History Press
Printed in Great Britain

CONTENTS

FOREWORD

I chose to write this book to document the role the area played during the Second World War, both as a reference tool and for documenting the history for future generations. Few towns can claim to have been as important to the greater war effort as Blackpool. The Fylde had no fewer than four operational airfields and was a key factor for training new recruits for the RAF. The area also played a more traditional role in the conflict, such as maintaining tourism, which allowed people to forget about the horrors of war (even if only for a short period) and heavy industry, with the Vickers factory churning out spectacular numbers of bomber aircraft.

The area has had its fair share of ups and downs, including the tragedies of the Freckleton and Central Station air disasters, which brought untold misery to those affected. There is also an element of mystery surrounding the fascinating 'People's Playground' story, in which Hitler had apparently earmarked the resort as a future National Socialist centre.

Whilst researching the book, I have uncovered many stories that I have found interesting and thought should be shared. The war played a crucial role in the development of the area and signs are still visible today if you know where to look. Remnants of the resort's wartime past still stand both tangibly, in the many pillboxes and structures, and intangibly, with the unseen legacy of some of the area's current major employers who owe their existence in the area to the Second World War. These include BAE Systems, Springfields Fuels Ltd (in Salwick and formerly British Nuclear Fuels Ltd) and the Department for Work and Pensions (DWP). For the purpose of this book, I have defined the area covered as the Fylde Coast. Areas included are Blackpool, Fleetwood, Lytham St Anne's, Kirkham, Over Wyre and rural Fylde. By documenting the exploits of the people who served, worked and lived in the area during the war my hope is that they will be remembered long into the future.

I hope you find reading the book as interesting as I have found writing it, and enjoy discovering the huge part that this small area of the Lancashire coastline played in the wider conflict.

Finally, I would like to thank everyone who contributed to the book, including the authors and enthusiasts who provided great reference material and the people that showed me support at every level. Special mention must go to my father, Andrew Ellis, who provided me with additional material as well as local historical knowledge gathered from growing up in the area (and also helped with some of the writing), and my mother, Ruth Ellis, who did all the proofreading and provided advice. Finally, I would like to thank everyone at The History Press who freely gave help and useful tips to this novice author. They also showed support in getting the project off the ground and the book would not have been possible without the publisher's support and experience.

INTRODUCTION

In 1939, an air of uncertainty hung over the country and the mood in Blackpool was no exception. The resort had experienced a poor holiday season as people awaited the outcome of Neville Chamberlain's ill-fated appeasement policy and the population feared what the future would bring. In Blackpool, preparations were being made to ready the population for war with local decision-makers planning to cope with the worst scenarios. The two greatest pre-war fears of gas attacks and devastating civilian bombings were prevalent, and there was real concern coming from the people 'in the know'. In response, the Government issued gas masks to everyone, warnings were everywhere and stocks of hundreds of thousands of death certificates were distributed around the country. Air-raid precaution leaflets were handed out as early as 1936. As tensions mounted and war became inevitable, the preparations moved up a gear: cardboard coffins were stockpiled at Raikes garage and some 2,000 air-raid shelters sprung up in the area, the promenade housing some of the biggest. These shelters provided accommodation for over 85,000 people and cost nearly £300,000 to build. Young men from the resort had to complete National Service and everyone was preparing for the worst. The Government encouraged flying clubs with Squires Gate and Stanley Park both having their own meetings. Odd radar structures sprang up in the area, which included the Blackpool Tower for a brief period along with a site at the back of St-Anne's-On-Sea. To add to the problems the winter of early 1939 was particularly bad and all the omens seemed to be pointing to a declaration of war materialising.

When war was finally declared the population sprang into action and civilian buildings were protected by sandbags filled on the beaches by volunteers. The Home Guard was formed along with Air Raid Precautions (ARP) teams. The ARP built a fire station in Bispham on Red Bank Road and had its training centre in a garage on the corner of Deansgate and Lytham Road in South Shore. Men enlisted voluntarily and were also called up for various services, some were to go on to the Continent to try to hold back Hitler's army before it overran France, others waited for the war to hit Britain. Many local

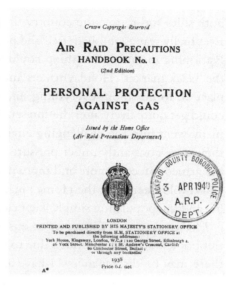

ARP book stamped by Blackpool County Borough Police.

volunteers made their way to the Far East where they would serve in the ill-fated early defence of the outposts of the British Empire. Precautionary measures were taken with road signs being blackened out to disorientate the Germans (although with a 500ft tower I think it wouldn't have taken even the most navigationally inept location finders long to realise they were in Blackpool). The pre-war building boom which saw many buildings such as the Derby Baths, the Opera House, the Odeon Cinema and Talbot Road bus station being built was immediately stopped as construction resources were diverted to war projects. Water tanks sprang up in the area as one major fear the Government had was that the nation's water supplies would be cut off if reservoir walls were cracked by Luftwaffe bombs. Many places were requisitioned for various different purposes. Evacuees started to flood into the resort from neighbouring cities such as Manchester, putting strains on local services as well as the families who agreed to accept them (although for some their residency would not last long). Women were put into jobs such as driving the town's famous trams to free up men for soldiering. Campaigns were launched in order to help the war, calling on civilians to donate money or goods, many took up the challenge and Revoe Park was used as an area to house scrap metal donations. It was a weird time as the 'phoney war' as it came to be known as was in full swing. Britain was at war but it hadn't yet been directly hit or experienced a significant loss of life. Time was needed by both sides and it gave the country time to prepare and get its ship in order. Eventually war established itself and people began to get used to the conflict. Rationing meant that nothing could be wasted and many locals turned to the 'black market'. Holidaymakers and soldiers on leave used the resort as a place to forget about everything, and the various entertainment buildings could get quite lively after the sun set. For residents hard work was necessary, many went into the challenging environment of the Vickers factory where they were constantly under pressure to perform. Others were drafted into the armed forces as more and more men were needed, others, who couldn't enlist, volunteered for the Home Guard. Eventually the war became a fact of life and the population simply 'kept calm and carried on'.

I have taken every measure to ensure that the information contained in this book is accurate although due to the unavailability of secondary sources there may be discrepancies. I have also recorded every source I used and made strenuous efforts to ensure no copyright has been compromised. I am indebted to all of these sources and the people who offered me help at every stage and provided information which helped to shape the book. I would welcome feedback on the book and any other information/sources or photos of the Fylde during the conflict to help keep the legacy alive.

CHAPTER I

RAF
SQUIRES GATE

Blackpool already had a long history of aviation before the start of the Second World War. The original airport to the south of the town (which would later become RAF Squires Gate and the modern-day Blackpool International Airport), was host to its, and indeed Lancashire's, first powered flight during an air show in October 1909. It was one of the first airstrips to open in the country and was a pioneer of regional aviation. The initial facilities were basic, relying on the flat land and its proximity to the resort to cater for small bi-planes, the sort made famous over the trenches of the First World War. It was also the site of the first official meeting of the Aero Club and held an early air show. With the public fascinated by the technology of the early planes, the show was attended by around 200,000 people. It was a showcase for the latest technology and attendees proudly flew flags during the show, consumed over 36,000 bottles of beer and some 500 hog roasts. The show included many pioneers of flight, most notably Henry Farman. The field initially ran pleasure flights in the area as well as being home to a small club for local pilots who wanted to get to grips with the unusual machines. As well as being one of the country's new airports, it saw other uses including life as a military hospital during the Great War and as a racetrack. Although the airport did eventually host some commercial flying activity, including direct flights to the Isle of Man that was mostly cut off from the mainland at that time and relied upon steam ferries, but eventually it lost out as the new council-backed municipal airport situated at Stanley Park gained favour. However, some direct flights to the Isle of Man still fly from the original airport to this day.

As an existing airfield with operational history, space to expand, situated near a large population and near (as the crow flies) to the target port city of Liverpool, it comes as no surprise that the airport was chosen as a Second World War RAF base. The site was requisitioned, along with almost all of the country's existing airfields, slightly before the outbreak of the conflict. Squires Gate, similar to Stanley Park, was also home to a flying club, which the RAF planners saw as a quick way to train enthusiasts ready for operational combat in the event of an invasion threat. It was men lured from the early flying clubs that were to become 'the few', who staved off the Luftwaffe during the precarious years of the Battle of Britain. Many of the older hands would be responsible for training pilots for both Fighter and Bomber Command, with many recruits undertaking their general training in various locations around the resort. At the outbreak of the war, many buildings were erected to bring the site up to operational standards, being initially run by the RAF Volunteer Reserve. These included numerous hangars, a control tower and accommodation for workers on the outskirts of the airfield. Existing buildings were used, some improved and some, like the old racecourse buildings, were simply used for storage. Four large metal Bellman hangars were built to house the planes safely; these could be erected quickly from flat-packs in order to get the airfields up and running as soon as possible. The speed of construction was quite staggering and included offices, arms/bomb storage facilities, air-raid shelters, photographic interpretation suites, an airfield defence office, staff 'NAAFI' quarters and numerous other buildings and, by the end of the construction spree, some 200 had been erected on the site. The large air traffic control tower is still in use today (although it has gone through some modernisation), which is situated in the centre of the airfield with a good view of the operations.

One of the biggest improvements to the site was the laying of three large runways in 1940, which were made out of bitumen in order to ease aircraft movements and allow larger planes to land, thus improving the sites capability. A golf course that bordered the site was built over to accommodate the full-length runway. The clubhouse from the old course was dismantled and moved to the Lytham Green Drive course where it formed part of that clubhouse. It was around this time that the field began to be referred to as RAF Squires Gate. Initially it was thought that the site would be used as a Coastal Command Centre, taking advantage of its situation on the Irish Sea coast, but it had numerous other uses with a heavy focus on training. It was also used as an operational night fighter station where it focused primarily on protecting the city of Liverpool, in particular its ports that were vital in landing 'lend/lease' equipment and much needed food and supplies into the country.

100 years of flying

FROM BLACKPOOL INTERNATIONAL

Modern airport sign highlights the airfield's illustrious history.

The airport, being an important site, needed to be protected both from the air and from the ground, for which anti-aircraft guns were placed near to the sand dunes and there was a concentration of pillboxes situated around the field. Other buildings sprang up from the airfield, including the Vickers aircraft factory situated further up Squires Gate Lane and the old Wood Street Mission holiday camp, which was used as accommodation, although mainly for billeting troops from the Manchester Regiment. Initially units were stationed at Squires Gate as part of a scheme to rotate and disperse them from other regions, particularly from the vulnerable southern airfields, which were seen as key targets for the Luftwaffe. These early squadron visitors (such as 63, 75, 215, and 256 Squadrons) were to form some of the units who fought tooth and nail against Hitler in the Battle of Britain in 1940.

The Coastal Command aircraft were used to patrol against German U-boats operating mainly in the Atlantic, subsequently, as the range of the aircraft improved, they would help protect convoys further afield. Convoys, particularly from Liverpool, travelled in the Irish Sea off the coast of the Fylde. Training was a big part of life, so much so that the land closest to Squires Gate Lane itself was given over to training facilities and numerous classroom buildings were erected at the site along with other training facilities. The west side of the airfield and adjacent to the railway line was a gunning range where moving targets would be towed for trainee pilots to practise on. With all this activity, a number of aircraft accidents were inevitable. An accident that is not that well known occurred when the pilot of a Fairey aircraft clipped the Squires Gate railway bridge when he lost his bearings during a practice session. The plane then crashed and three people lost their lives in the incident. The three aircraft that flew in formation before the Blackpool Central Station disaster had also set off from the airfield.

Blackpool Airport runway with the old Pontins Holiday Camp buildings in the foreground.

Different training courses were taken at the site, including photographic reconnaissance (which operated the famous Spitfire aircraft), observation and navigation schools and flying practice. Some of the schools that used the airport were the Nos 2 and 3 Schools of General Reconnaissance and the No. 3 School of Technical Training.

The site was also operational for flying missions in the greater arena of the war. Night fighters, protecting Merseyside, Liverpool and the North West were based at the site. The airfield was often used as a satellite site for squadrons based at other fields in the North West, such as Speke, Burtonwood etc., to allow them wider coverage of the area. In late 1940, 96 Squadron sent a detachment of aircraft to the field and German aircraft were shot down by planes based in Blackpool. As well as British squadrons, a Polish squadron (No. 308) formed at Squires Gate (the Polish Air Force being based in the town centre), which gave the field an international flavour. As a recognised operational field, other aircraft in trouble could land at the site. One of the more notable landings was when the sole surviving bomber touched down after a daring raid at the MAN diesel factory in Germany, for which some of the crew were rewarded for their bravery. The airfield was a part of local life and most people found it simply exciting. A wide array of differing aircraft used the site making it a Mecca for plane spotters and the local children. It did bring its problems though, as it could be quite noisy and had to operate at night, as well as having the habit of attracting unwanted German attention. Nearly a hundred bombs were dropped at the site, although the number could have been much higher as and evidence has been uncovered that the Germans were aware of the runways and factory buildings. One bombing raid happened when a lone German bomber tailed a night fighter back as it landed, and then let its bomb loose over the central runways. Nearby streets, including Faringdon Avenue and Squires Gate Lane, did suffer minor bomb damage. As a token gesture of the local desire to help the site, money was raised to purchase aircraft for use by the RAF. Enough was raised to buy three spitfires, which took the town's motto ('Progress' 1, 2 & 3), and a lavish ceremony took place that helped bridge the gap between the local community and the airfield.

In 1940, the site was briefly used by larger transport planes as part of an air convoy route with North America. Lockheed Liberator aircraft flew regularly between Squires Gate and Montreal in Canada to bring back vital supplies for the British.

After a very busy and effective wartime operation, Squires Gate airfield was handed back to civilian usage in August 1946 and the RAF moved out. The airport is now very busy and has regular flights to the Isle of Man, Ireland and the Continent, continuing its rich tradition of aviation.

CHAPTER 2

THE VICKERS ARMSTRONG FACTORY AT SQUIRES GATE

The site, which is situated next to the modern-day Blackpool Airport – or RAF Squires Gate as it was known during the Second World War – was one of the largest aircraft manufacturing centres in the country. It was a huge complex, over 1,500,000 square feet, on the edge of town, which hired large numbers of local workers, often women, to build the fearsome Wellington bomber. It was the centre of large-scale production and many of the town's other buildings were used as satellite sites. Some of the most notable used for production were the Talbot Road bus station, Stanley Park Aerodrome and Blackpool Pleasure Beach, each specialising in its own part of the production process. The site was critical in respect of the volume of aircraft produced for Bomber Command. The factory churned out just short of 3,000 of the large bombers (some references show even higher production numbers) which helped turn the tide of the war and secure Allied victory. At its operational peak the factory produced over 100 bombers a month to be put into service by the RAF. The average time it took to build a plane was around 60 hours more than other models as it was hard to assemble. It used many different materials that had to be brought into Blackpool including metal, wood and linen. Most people have heard of the Wellington bomber. It was the only aircraft to be produced for the duration of the war and it is said that over 20 per cent of all the Wellington bombers made were at Squires Gate. The shadow sites in the area highlight how critical the operation was to the wider conflict and indeed Bomber Command.

The former Vickers Armstrong factory at Squires Gate.

The site was earmarked in the early stages as a potential shadow factory for the Weybridge site, and it was decided that a large factory should be purpose-built for production adjacent to the already operational airfield. Plane production commenced with parts brought in from the Weybridge site even before the factory construction was complete – starting in temporary hangars. During construction the roof collapsed and the site had its first casualties with six people being killed (there is a detailed document about the accident stored in the National Archives should you wish to have more information). The large factory, which still stands today on Squires Gate Lane and has a recognisable roof, was once home to the simultaneous production of multiple aircraft by a variety of workers at any one time. Specialist machines were erected including drilling apparatus, overhead cranes to transport the planes down the production line, large metal lathes, and riveting machines. The noise and heat must have been immense and conditions hard. Due to the size of the site, it needed railway access and so track was laid, which has since been concreted over, to connect the factory to the South Fylde branch line near to Squires Gate station. Many local women were put into an alien setting along with school leavers and other youngsters, the minimum age being 16 years old to work on the floor. As well as manual labour, a variety of 'white collar' roles were also required to run the factory including senior and junior management, administration staff, switchboard operators, human resource specialists, etc., who were mostly recruited from the local area.

The Wellington bomber was a large, medium range, twin-engined bomber that operated on mainly night-time bombing raids. It slowly fell out of favour towards the end of the war, although it played a pivotal role in anti-submarine warfare (often being kitted out with radar and mine detection apparatus). The planes served in numerous different operations from fabled anti-VI raids to the harrowing flattening of German cities. Places like Cologne suffered at the hands of such planes when the city was demolished in the first 1,000 bomber raid, the majority of which were Wellington bombers. The local workers certainly were not to blame for the havoc being caused by the fruits of their labours but it is hard to argue in favour of carpet-bombing now, and we have to recognise that Blackpool did play a role in this. The planes built in the town were piloted by many different nations, including the Free French, Polish (the Polish HQ was located on Talbot Road) and South Africans. It saw operations all over the world being notably effective in the North African campaign and the Allied fight in the Middle East.

The factory provided welcome permanent work for many in the area both in the factory itself and at ancillary sites around the town. After the depression of the 1930s and the town's traditional reliance on low paid seasonal wages, the work was welcome and money could be made. You had to work hard and, as with most war production, workers, often women (including my grand-mother who worked in the offices at the factory), had to work long hours in a target-driven environment. Workers were told the faster they worked the

Modern photograph of what was once the Vickers Armstrong factory.

quicker the war would be over and there was some truth in this statement. At its peak, over 10,000 people worked at the site, some were even bussed in from East Lancashire to meet the demand. The conditions were hard and some of the jobs were dangerous and quite skilled (if a little repetitive). The factory manufactured all parts of the bomber and different workers specialised in different things. At shift change hundreds of bicycles would flood the nearby roads, such as St Anne's Road (then longer than it is now), Squires Gate Lane and Highfield Road, and would have been quite a sight to any observers.

To view the Vickers factory as simply Squires Gate would not be appropriate. The town as a whole became linked to the factory itself with many satellite sites acting as spin offs from the main factory. Some of these sites were unique to Blackpool including the Pleasure Beach, where sheds that had previously been used to build and repair the rides were converted to working factory space. In particular, the old maintenance sheds now situated at the back of the site were used to produce gunning turrets. To have people enjoying much needed wartime respite on the rides, such as the Big Dipper and Grand National, so close to locals churning out parts in an intense war production environment could not have occurred anywhere other than in Blackpool. These activities illustrated some of the most important roles the resort played during this troubled time.

Talbot Road bus station was also used by the factory. As production increased, more space was needed and the floors above the ground level once used by the buses had large machines installed and these were utilised to make parts. Workers had to get the pieces needed for production from the offices at the top of the building and then account for each piece. By workers having to report for each new part the management could identify anyone that was not pulling their weight – even toilet breaks were monitored. Not working as hard as you could was considered a bad effort and very un-British. The factory and its sites had very little problems with production being interrupted by worker grievances such as strikes and 'go slows', as the locals just wanted to do anything they could to help the greater cause. However, other industries did suffer elsewhere across the country from this, particularly the shipyards and mining. The factory also brought war production to the centre of the town near to the North Station, so access was good.

Another site used by the factory was the old coach-building firm of H.V. Burlingham (the predecessor of the Marton Duple coaches operation), based just off Preston New Road in Marton. Production of peacetime coaches was halted and the buildings were requisitioned to support bomber production. The main purpose of this site was to build airframes to be transported to

Squires Gate. The existing workers were used for such tasks as they dealt with metal sheets in the production of the classical coaches and were good at producing the important airframes needed for the large bombers. The art of coach building did not end completely though and one of the Burlingham sites on Newhouse Road (just off Vicarage Lane, near the old Oxford pub) continued to make coaches, although they were heavily adapted for war uses. They produced several different vehicles including mobile canteens for the army using Austin Dodgers as the basis for their completion. The old tram sheds, also in Marton, were used to build the wings of the planes before they were driven to Squires Gate for final assembly. The old Ribble bus garage on Devonshire Road produced fuel tanks for the bombers. Quite a few other buildings in the town worked as smaller premises as annexes to the Squires Gate factory and its huge scale. Another site commandeered by the factory was the old bus depot that used to stand on Devonshire Road, again it had a speciality – its mechanical past meant that it was well equipped to produce fuel tanks. With all these sites working together production was quick; on one occasion in 1942 approximately 300 bombers had to be stored on the beach because they were awaiting installation of a propeller and had to be moved from the factory as nothing could stop the work. It must have been an amazing sight to see.

The most famous satellite site though must have been the airfield at Stanley Park, now used by Blackpool Zoo and the De Vere Hotel and golf course. It was the largest of the satellite sites and planes were actually built to completion there. The site had taken control of a large aerodrome that had opened in the 1930s, and was used as the main municipal airport for the resort just before the outbreak of war. It even had an operational runway as well as many large hangars that could be utilised by the staff for production purposes. Many local firms operated on the frames and combined parts shipped in and pieced together at Stanley Park. The area was chosen because despite being an airfield it had not been properly utilised as such because it was not really fit for purpose. It was also capable of dispersing production from the main factory should the latter be 'taken out' by enemy activity. Interestingly, the bomber built at the site could take off from there but the runway was too small for them to land. Many one-way flights took off as the bombers came off the production line, most simply flying the short hop to Squires Gate. The airfield was improved with meshing and the planes could only just take off with low fuel without sinking into the sodden ground. Production was self-contained and was quite low in the grand scheme of things, with around five planes being churned out each week, but it all added to the production numbers that could be credited to the local workers.

Gathered workers and dignitaries from around the area saw the last Wellington flight out of the town in October 1945, and they must have been relieved, hoping for a rest and probably a little bit sad. What is for sure is that their hard work helped the Allies win the war.

The factory continued work after the conflict, providing much-needed jobs and carrying on a specialist local skill in aircraft production that continues to this day. Immediately after the war, the site was used to build aluminium homes as part of the social improvements made during Clement Atlee's premiership. For a short time the site was also used for the repair of government cars, although it was hundreds rather than thousands that worked at the site as Britain had to pay for its expensive war. There were some heated debates in the House of Commons at the time about the use of the site involving local MPs and Harold Macmillan (then in charge of housing) and it eventually became operational making fighter jets for the future anti-communist military endeavours. The Hawker aircraft company took over the site and eventually hired around 5,000 locals, providing much-needed jobs and bringing back a busy factory floor. Aircraft production finally ceased in the late 1950s and the site is now largely used for warehousing.

CHAPTER 3

EDUCATION
AND
EVACUEES

Thanks to the great fear of heavy and sustained Axis bombing, a decision was taken to evacuate children from large cities in order to protect them. This meant that Blackpool, which was not deemed as much of a target, would take in many young children and families. The operation was well planned with teachers and civil servants helping to make the transition as easy as possible. It was a stressful time for everyone but none more so than for the young children who were often torn away from their families and friends. The majority of the evacuees arrived via train and they were processed in a centre on Whitegate Drive. Many houses in the resort took in the children and often it was hard for all involved. The majority of the children who came to the area were from the industrial city of Manchester, although there was also a sizeable number from Merseyside and even the capital. The new influx caused a strain on many services, with the greatest affected being the schools. Many schools were partnered with inner-city counterparts and often there was simply not enough space for everyone to co-exist.

The allocation of children to host families was a crude affair with buses bringing the kids down the streets, simply dropping them off with a family who had signed up to taking them in. For some this was a happy time and a number of the evacuated children had never seen the sea before and for some Blackpool would have been an adventure. For others, who were homesick or did not like their new families, it could be very traumatic. Many of the initial arrivals soon went home after the bombing of the cities did not reach the levels feared. Others stayed longer and evacuees came to the area throughout the war, often after devastating bombing raids. Blackpool was host to over 35,000 children as well as single mothers and others considered vulnerable. In fact, the area took in a few children who would go on to be famous, most notably Barbara Windsor who moved to the resort to avoid the East London blitz and went on to attend Norbreck Primary School for a brief period. Another piece of local trivia is that Ricky Tomlinson was born in the resort as his mother's family moved to the Cleveleys area from Merseyside during the conflict and he was raised in the area.

A number of families who had spare rooms chose to take in children and the incomers were distributed all around the Fylde Coast in all manner of surroundings. Most people just wanted to do their bit, some were buoyed on by propaganda and some simply did not want to appear bad in front of their neighbours. Whatever the reason, it was a funny time for everyone involved and all sides had to adjust. As well as houses, many of the resort's thousands of bedsits were turned over to accommodate the evacuees.

The local schools had to make room suddenly for a large influx of new pupils, all of whom needed to keep up to date with the curriculum. The arrangements to manage this mass exodus from the cities started before the war was officially declared. Many teachers, including those in the area, had their traditional summer holiday cut short to help with the administration of the evacuation plans should total war occur. The fact that the mammoth operation ran largely without a hiccup was thanks to this forward planning. On numerous occasions the country proved it was more than capable of forward planning, such as with radar, utilisation of labour etc., something the opposition often failed to accredit. The teachers deserve to be recognised for the effort they put in, most were appointed 'assistant billeting officers' and lists of potential movements were completed long before Hitler's tanks rolled over the Polish border. The children were moved as soon as war was declared, the Government did not hang around and, for approximately two weeks, houses and families were paired up with evacuees.

Pressure abated after a large number of the children moved back to the un-bombed towns they came from, the area did however continue to open its doors to those infants in danger.

A list of school pairings:

St Joseph's School, Blackpool with de La Salle College, Merseyside
Palatine School, Blackpool (not the current school of that name) with Manchester Grammar School

Waterloo School, South Shore took in pupils from Lily Infants School, Manchester

St John's School, Town Centre with John Street School, inner-city Salford

Collegiate School in Highfurlong, Blackpool with Manchester Central High School for Girls

Thornton Cleveleys School with Cavendish Senior and Didsbury Central schools, Manchester

King Edward School, Lytham took in children from South East London

Queen Mary School, Lytham took in pupils from Levenshulme, South Manchester and from Runcorn

Fleetwood Grammar School took in pupils from Widnes

Although not all schools in the area were paired, most took in the evacuees at the start of the war. Thames School had pupils from Liverpool, and Revoe School had children from a number of different areas. So much so that the latter had to use an old church hall on Salthouse Avenue, near to what is now the cinema complex, as an annex. Many of the schools lacked the space to cope and many divided the day between the paired school and their existing pupils. Days often ran from 9 a.m. to 1 p.m. and from 2 p.m. to 5.30 p.m. so that everyone could get a decent education. The newcomers were settled as well as possible bearing in mind the circumstances. Many took to the local parks and others were taken for a walk along the beach. The local children played a role too as many tried to comfort the displaced youngsters and games of football with Manchester versus Blackpool were common on the streets. Some schools had to close altogether, Rossall for instance moved all its pupils to the Lake District as the school was used by civil servants for the early years.

Even after the majority of the evacuees had moved back, movements of children to and from the area ebbed and flowed with events. For instance, Collegiate School took in whole classes from Stretford High school in West Manchester. The reason for this was that the area was a target for heavy bombing thanks to its close proximity to the industrial areas of Trafford Park and the docks on the Manchester Ship Canal. The school moved into the resort in 1943 after damage to its surrounding area. As well as evacuees, schools had to help with settling children down and provide a normal environment for them to escape to. Leisure was a big part of the curriculum during the war and sports were encouraged as a way of releasing tension. The war was still mentioned and propaganda and advice given to the children during classes. Pupils of the various secondary schools would often be required to lend a helping hand on allotments and school fields, which had been turned over to crop growing together with inland farms by way of feeding a nation under rationing. When the pupils grew up and left school many were drafted into the army or made Bevin Boys or Land Girls.

The 1975 drama *The Evacuees*, written by Jack Rosenthal, was based on evacuees' experiences after moving to the resort during the conflict. It was supposedly based on his experiences as an evacuee and the film chronicles two Jewish boys from war torn Manchester trying to get to grips with the strange surroundings. It was mainly filmed around Lytham St Anne's and starred Jack's wife, Maureen Lipman. The film was a critical success and won many awards.

CHAPTER 4

TOURISM
DURING THE WAR

Prior to the outbreak of war in 1939, Blackpool was prospering and new buildings including the famous Derby Baths, the Odeon Cinema (now renowned Funny Girls revue bar), a new Opera House and Talbot Road bus station were all opened in the year. Progress was of course halted by the hostilities. The resort then sprang into action and went from 'fun and frolics' to serious work overnight (although there was still plenty of wartime fun to be had). On 3 September 1939, two days after the declaration of war, a national ban on entertainment was announced thus temporary ending the party atmosphere. This started an unusual period in the resort's economic history as some things, such as the illuminations, did not take place at all during the war years, but some attractions experienced an increase in visitor numbers. It was a time of great uncertainty, as people did not know what to expect.

Towards the end of 1939, there was a great unknown in Britain, as people did not know how the war would pan out, the greatest fears being that of extensive civilian bombing and gas attacks, which would of course have a disastrous effect on tourism in the resort. There were many influxes of people to the town when the nation's evacuation plans were implemented and this had a huge affect on the numerous boarding houses and hotels, which soon became full with the Government providing payment for each evacuee. The evacuation itself was planned far in advance and was implemented very quickly with the help of civil servants and teachers, and masses of people were transported around the country with the best intentions of saving lives. The operation ran smoothly (it was one of the first glimpses of the British organisational ability during the war) and with so many spare rooms, Blackpool was a busy destination. This first evacuation wave was short because it was believed that the war would not last long and was soon labelled the 'phoney war', so with a lack of civilian bombing the majority returned home. Although some returned to the resort as bombing increased at a later stage.

Blackpool demonstrated its ability to receive people and it was taken as a sign that the tourism would be replaced and places would be kept busy. The illuminations did not shine in 1939, although they were all ready to go. Just a day before war was declared, they had a trial run with, ironically, a large searchlight shining from the top of the tower over the town – soon real searchlights would be seen in the skies over the resort. Obviously, with the Luftwaffe buzzing overhead, the lights would have identified the resort to unwanted enemy attention and so it is not surprising that they were left switched off. Typical of the 'make do' attitude of the town's accommodation providers, many a landlady installed coloured bulbs behind the blackouts to try and imitate the famous lights and restore pre-war normality. Despite the victory, the illuminations themselves did not shine again until 1949 because of energy shortages, although they were doubtless better appreciated the first time they shone post-war.

Probably the key to the resort staying busy was the influx of military personnel, particularly the RAF, and that of Government officials. The resort was chosen for such relocations for a number of reasons but availability of rooms was a key factor. Businesses in Blackpool were lucky thanks to its location, as the resorts on the more vulnerable east coast suffered more from attacks, particularly in the South, and remained closed for business during the entire war. Blackpool was deemed by authorities to be at low risk of attack and thus made a great place to send government departments who were under fire in the capital and other large cities. In fact, most of the large hotels were predominantly commandeered by the Government, including the Imperial Hotel, which was used by the Inland Revenue (now part of HMRC) and the Ministry of Agriculture and Fisheries, and the Kimberley Hotel on South Promenade, which was converted into a maternity hospital with many births being recorded there. Squires Gate holiday camp was used for a variety of purposes, most famously as HMS Prithibian, accommodation for the Royal Navy. One of the largest movers was the Department of Health, who used many hotels together with Rossall School during the war. The Pensions Office moved initially to Cleveleys Hydro before being relocated to a new site built on Warbreck Hill, but also used a number of the town's hotels. Warbreck Hill is still used by the Department for Work and

Pensions to this day and the majority of modern government sites in the town owe their existence to these wartime relocations.

Another legacy of Blackpool's accommodation space is the Welfare State itself. Many historians would regard this as one of the greatest outcomes of the war, as the population demanded an improvement in general conditions and welfare provisions. One thing that is not as well known is that the hard working economists and civil servants tasked with organising this great welfare system did so in the town's many holiday rooms. Andrew Marr mentions the resort's role in this in his *History of Modern Britain* television programme and associated book. In total, over 4,000 civil servants were moved to the resort during the early stages of the war in a variety of roles. It is important to view Blackpool's room capacity and its ability to provide workspace as a national resource, which the Government utilised effectively for the country's benefit.

Blackpool was probably the biggest seaside resort to be used for war work but not the only one, for example, the Isle of Man was famous as a prisoner of war internment camp. Manx boarding houses were used to hold prisoners for the duration of the war and one prisoner originally incarcerated there was Charlie Cairoli, who went on to become the most famous clown at the Blackpool Tower Circus (he was eventually released with a little help from a French passport). Many of the prisoners who went to the Isle of Man did so via the resort, often spending a night in Blackpool before being shipped off from the Lancashire ports including up the promenade at Fleetwood.

Front cover of a souvenir postcard booklet (c.1910), which unusually shows swastikas as part of its design.

The largest contingent of people visiting the area came not from civil servants but from military personnel, in particular the RAF, who sent most of its recruits to the resort for basic training. Attracted by the numerous rooms and local facilities, huge numbers came through the resort for training. A total of 769,673 people were trained in the resort by the RAF, with up to 50,000 people there at any one time. The working day was hard but most of the recruits let their hair down at night and when on leave, which ensured that the local attractions were kept busy and business was good; most businesses followed the national example and offered a discount for those serving in the military forces. It wasn't just the hotels the RAF utilised, as public spaces were requisitioned as well. Most famously, they used the expanse of the Winter Gardens complex but other tourist favourites such as North Pier and the Blackpool Tower were also requisitioned. The ballroom played host to gruelling physical activities during the day and dances in the evening; nearly all of the rooms were occupied for training, exercises and lectures.

In addition to the Winter Gardens, the Pleasure Beach used its ride workshops to produce small components for the Wellington bombers being assembled at Squires Gate. The Pleasure Beach still managed to open, unusually, all year round as the influx of military personnel and others challenged the resort's reliance on seasonality, which still plagues the resort's employment opportunities. As people got used to the war, in the early 1940s, tourism began to pick up and room shortages were common due to the numbers of personnel and visitors choosing the resort. Even to this day, a full Blackpool is deemed a successful Blackpool and many a business would love to have visitor numbers as high as they were during the war, though not under the same circumstances. Credit and remembrance should be shown to the tourist establishments and workers who did their bit for the war effort.

Largely, the resort's changes ran smoothly, although there were a few hiccups. For instance, some landladies thought that the amount the Government was giving for their rooms left them out of pocket as the rates were seen as less than the going 'tourist' rate. Some hotels had to turn down regular visitors as rooms were being used by soldiers and workers. The jostle between tourist and worker for space occasionally flared up and on one occasion, in 1943, a tense strike was held by civil service workers who blocked the tram tracks, as they wanted priority on the transport system over tourists. Another problem for the tourist industry was the lack of available staff, with most being commandeered to work in war factories. Many of those employed were women. Nazi ideology did not allow for women in the workplace and the nation's utilisation of workers formulated by people like William 'Max' Aitken (Lord Beaverbrook), was an important national tool in the fight.

Despite the huge impact the war had on tourism, Blackpool's position was quite good and when the lucrative coach tours were stopped because of petrol rationing in 1942, the resort survived in an untraditional way as the tourist venues found alternative customers from the pool of new temporary residents. When tourists did come to the area they often had to bring their own rationed foods such as butter, sugar and eggs, which would be handed over at the bed and breakfasts to be cooked by the landladies. The war brought some benefits to the area from abroad as large numbers of Americans were based in the town and surrounding areas, with Freckleton even being known as 'Little America'. Other armed forces were also represented by Free French or Polish soldiers coming to the resort during their leave. This led to the owner of the Pleasure Beach, Leonard Thompson saying that '... entertainment is about the only commodity that isn't rationed'.

In real terms Blackpool served as a good place to relax, let your hair down and forget about the war , if only for a short period of time. It offered a familiar holiday in an unfamiliar time and this was good for the morale of the nation.

CHAPTER 5

TRAINING
THE RAF

Arguably, Blackpool's largest and most important role played in the conquest was to train raw RAF recruits into becoming competent military men. The resort was selected as suitable for such a large training site for a number of reasons. Most significantly, huge numbers of recruits had to be housed for the duration of their training and Blackpool with its large number of hotel rooms was one of the only locations in the country that could accommodate them. With requisitioning laws giving the Government widespread powers, and the number of beds in the resort reportedly eclipsing the number available in Portugal as a whole, a plan was set in motion to make the establishment of a training base possible. Utilising existing room capacity in the resort meant that expensive accommodation blocks did not have to be erected and precious materials could be saved. Time was also a factor as recruits needed to be operational quickly, particularly in the early days, to protect the country.

Although it is likely that the availability of accommodation was the main reason the RAF chose Blackpool, it was not the only factor. The large open promenades were ideal for physical training and marching practise, with recruits being put through their paces by their instructors up and down the Golden Mile. Physical training was a key part of the course as people needed to be fit, but it also instilled a sense of discipline into the recruits, introducing them to the military way of life and turning them into professionals. Blackpool was also accessible, being situated close enough to main population areas without being over exposed to a possible German attack, and with a transport infrastructure (from the trains to the trams) that regularly proved itself capable of handling large numbers of tourists. The other resorts on the east and south coast, such as Skegness and Brighton, were too exposed to the possibility of invasion and attack for an operation of such national importance to be mounted there.

Blackpool had plenty of suitable buildings that were needed for classrooms and large exhibition buildings were sought for the purpose. The Winter Gardens fitted the description well with great areas of floor space along with a whole series of separate rooms that could be used for the simultaneous teaching of several different subjects at any one time. The surrounding airfields were also an attractive prospect for RAF commanders, thus allowing trainee pilots some practical experience local to the main training area. Blackpool had a major military airport at Squires Gate, which was used in part for training pilots. RAF mechanics and ground crew received their technical training in and around Kirkham, although many received basic training in the resort. When you factor together all these pieces, Blackpool was really the obvious choice.

The effect that the influx of huge numbers of recruits had on the town cannot be underestimated, and Blackpool was streaming with members of military forces from all over the world. The increase in population was good for business and all fears of a poor holiday seasons resulting from the war were gone. The calendar positioning of a traditional season was irrelevant as the war was all year round. The boarding houses were full, with each owner receiving a fee for accommodating personnel as with evacuees. Spirits were generally high, although there were some rumblings, as loyal customers had to be turned away in favour of recruits. Friction occurred but the town generally took to its new role well.

Basic training lasted for around six weeks. As one set were turned out fully trained and operational, another set of rookies arrived to take their place, and this continued for many years during the worst of the conflict.

The training was not easy, especially for young people – Blackpool was apparently unforgiving as were the trainers. In particular, the drill sergeants were feared by the recruits as they gave out stern directions and, if necessary, stern discipline. A command hierarchy was formed with the trainees at the bottom, the speed and quality of the training being monitored and reported up through the line of management. A full command structure was established at the base and ran the operation so everyone had to answer to someone all the way up to the top echelons of the RAF and Government, such was the importance of the training. Blackpool can be very wet and the Irish Sea winds can be unforgiving at the best of times, so the conditions faced in training must have been extremely challenging.

Many different classes were taught in the Winter Gardens, the purpose of which was to mould the attendees from novices into experts. The building's size was a large factor in the decision and it came as no surprise because the the Admiralty had previously used the premises during the Great War. As well as technical training, propaganda was also important, so that soldiers knew the reasons why they were fighting in the war. Britain's propaganda was intended to improve determination and loyalty to the greater humanitarian cause. The ballroom at the Winter Gardens was used for physical exercise, the warren of other rooms were turned into makeshift lecture rooms, cinemas and practical work areas. The vast space of the Olympia Hall was used to teach Morse code and after their lessons, the recruits would take a test in a room above the old Burtons tailor's shop on Church Street. The horseshoe shaped arena in the complex was used to pay out the recruits' wages, and large sums of money were handled there. By day, the complex was very much a work space but by night it was transformed into an area of leisure – the grand dances held there were legendary and many a marriage owes its origins to these jaunts.

Other buildings besides those at the Winter Gardens were used and had specific roles to play. The recruits were taken once a week to the newly opened Derby Baths for a group shower. Radio operators were trained in the buildings and sheds of the Rigby Road bus depot, which housed a radio school. Palatine Road was used by the No. 2 Photography School to teach shooting and interpreting skills and, interestingly, photography is still taught in the area on the Blackpool and Fylde College campus situated there. To teach the course, large metal Nissen huts were built behind the then newly built college buildings to act as temporary classrooms. Even the Bloomfield Road pitch was used for the dreaded 'square bashing' (incidentally, Stanley Matthews was an RAF physical training instructor, which is probably why he played on into his fifties). The tranquil surroundings of Stanley Park were even used for practising throwing grenades! North Pier, which had a large part of it missing so it couldn't be used to land enemy troops, was also heavily used by the RAF.

With the North Pier and Winter Gardens being used, it was soon the Blackpool Tower's turn to play a role. The famous Tower Ballroom was used for aerobics classes, and the Tower Circus went from being the home of Charlie Cairoli and elephants to housing artillery lectures thanks to its vast seating capacity. Blackpool Cricket Club was also commandeered by the RAF and used for more physical training activities. The RAF built a large hangar at the site and the recruits had a successful cricket team, which shared the grounds with the local teams. RAF Squires Gate was used for more practical training as it had a bombing/target range, it too had classroom space and hosted photographic recognition classes. The list of venues appropriated by the RAF in the locality is very long with many other smaller buildings performing less significant roles. At the end of their training recruits had to complete an assault course before they were allowed to 'pass out'. Naturally, after finishing their training, with the knowledge that they had both completed something worthwhile and wouldn't have to run in the Irish Sea rain again, recruits were in the mood for a party and many a celebration drink was imbibed in the pubs around the resort.

We think of the RAF as 'The few' but Blackpool training provided people for Fighter and Bomber Command as well as all the jobs on the ground and in between. A 1,000 bomber raid needed thousands of trained men to enable it and was a continuous need. As the American 'lend lease' planes arrived in convoy, often through Scottish docks, they needed to be manned and Blackpool was called upon to get the ball rolling. D–Day was another huge undertaking, the largest military operation in history, and many planes were used which all needed crew. When the Americans joined the war in 1941, they were also seen in the resort. They behaved and marched in a completely differently way to the local troops and were viewed with humour by the British.

In 1942, a Polish technical training school was formed. The head of the Polish Air Force was based at the town's Lansdowne Hotel to be close to their headquarters. The numbers of Polish men in the resort meant that the Pleasure Beach translated all of its signs into Polish to cater for the visitors. They had their own hangouts and Hornby Road was a hotspot with the White Eagle officers' club situated there. The legacy still lasts to this day as many remained in the resort after the war because it was more favourable than Poland under Russian control. A Polish Club remained on Hornby Road until 1999 (when the three remaining Polish war veterans retired) and the recent wave of Polish immigrants was most certainly not the first into the resort. Other buildings in Blackpool town centre requisitioned for training purposes also included the Deacons Bank chambers building on Talbot Square, which became the No. 3 Training School. Talbot Road was thriving with military personnel and vehicles throughout the war. Blackpool-trained men who served in all of the major conflicts, battles and arenas of the war.

Slowly over time, the training operations began to run more and more efficiently as the area and the commanders became experts and evolved their various techniques. They provided a much-needed skilled resource for the war effort. This level of efficiency was vital because if the operation had not run smoothly and produced the numbers of men required (for all the different nationalities based in the area), the Allies could have lost the war. The effective utilisation of the whole of the population's labour resources for both military and civilian work was probably the main reason Britain survived the war and emerged triumphant.

CHAPTER 6

THE PEOPLE'S PLAYGROUND

This truly astonishing story was only recently uncovered during a historian's visit to Germany in 2007. The story broke in 2009 and attracted significant media interest nationwide. The initial documents were maps and aerial photographs, as well as instructions reportedly from Hitler to preserve the resort. It was odd that Blackpool had escaped bombing even though it played a pivotal role in Britain's war effort, which should have made it an attractive target for German Bomber Command. Despite having two airfields in Blackpool (RAF Stanley Park and RAF Squires Gate) and two on the Fylde (RAF Warton and HMS Nightjar), a huge aircraft factory, an ammunitions factory and a large RAF training centre, the town, which was not small in population particularly during the seasonal influxes, escaped a deliberate and concentrated bombing raid. The rationale behind this was a mystery, until these documents helped provide the answer, or so it seems.

Blackpool was to be left untouched and used as a 'people's playground' for the Germans. Blackpool was to play a huge role if the German's invaded, particularly in terms of propoganda. The plan included an invasion by German paratroopers to capture the resort intact and for them to 'goose-step' northwards along the promenade and, in the event of success, the swastika flying over Blackpool tower for the whole town and press to see; surely an opportunity that Joseph Goebbels and the propaganda ministry would have relished? The tower is a highly recognised symbol, particularly for northern Britain, and is known worldwide. Photographs of a swastika swaying 520ft high in the Irish Sea wind would surely have been some of the most iconic shots ever taken, akin to the famous pictures of Hitler sightseeing on the Eiffel tower in Paris, and no doubt would have dented the morale of a fighting Britain. The German reconnaissance photos show many of Blackpool's unmistakable landmarks, such as the piers and tower, as well as Stanley Park and the unique pattern of the Italian garden footpaths. The footpaths were to play a key role in the air-mounted landings, because they could be seen clearly from above and act as a compass point. It is strange that such a feature used for leisure even to this day and seemingly so insignificant would be seen, analysed and used by German Command many miles away, emphasising the new technologies and ways of thinking used in the conflict.

In 1940, the War Office issued some of the maps and photos that were recovered from an old German military base. These originated as part of a wide German reconnaissance effort, and had all the major landmarks, including what were Blackpool Central Station and the South Shore Lido, marked. It suggests the Germans were aware of the importance of the resort as a military venue, and that the Luftwaffe had shown an interest in the town. South Pier was also marked but as 'Victoria Pier'.

Elaine Smith, Chairman of Blackpool Civic Trust, said of the plans:

> These maps will be the source of much interest particularly to those who lived here (Blackpool) through the Second World War … It had been known that Hitler intended to use Blackpool as his personal playground after what he hoped to be a successful invasion and the war ended … We did escape a lot of the bombing despite the fact so many troops were in the town and there were major aircraft manufacturing factories here … He probably wanted to keep the resort as it was so he could enjoy it as Chancellor of Britain.

It is well known that the Germans were interested in leisure time and they had executed plans for their own Nazi seaside resort. The town of Prora on the German Baltic Coast might offer an example of what Blackpool could have expected if the invasion had taken place, and of what a Nazi resort would be like. Prora is said to have taken a lot of inspiration from British resorts and the popular holiday camps in particular. Many German ideals were implemented in providing cheap accommodation for the workers to enjoy good 'Aryan family fun', which was seen as essential in the planning of the resort. The town of Prora itself never reached the standard Hitler had proposed. He envisaged the largest sized resort, but it was not possible, particularly with construction workers being diverted to war work. He planned a town with big identical buildings in unified blocks, with lots of activities, including theatres and operas, available. Some buildings remain to this day and are some of the only examples of Third Reich architecture in existence. It is, therefore, very possible that this is what Hitler had in mind when trying to preserve Blackpool. As well as bespoke buildings, activities such as group exercise would have been planned as can be seen in many of the Nazi propaganda films.

Unfortunately, the discovery of the documents serves to create more questions than answers, which is often the case with new uninterpreted historical data. The plans and data, particularly as presented in the national press, were not in any great level of detail. The images and documents uncovered serve an important purpose in explaining the lack of bombing activity, but the full German plan for the resort is unknown.

CHAPTER 7

TRANSITION OF LABOUR AND THE WELFARE STATE

With London at risk, it was decided that to safeguard the nation's important services, government departments needed to be relocated. The new locations needed to be out of the range of large bombers and sustained German raids. Resorts situated on the south and east coasts were considered too close to the Continent, and so the north west coast was the obvious choice. The legacy of this move is still with us today and the Department for Work and Pensions (DWP), which for years was the area's largest employer, owes its roots in the area to the conflict. Many a future job opportunity was carved out by the Government's decision to relocate departments, to the coast in the early stages of the war, in particular the Ministry of Pensions. The modern DWP sites of Norcross, Warbreck Hill and Moorland Road in St Anne's all began life in the war period. Some have recently closed for staff to be moved to modern offices at Peel Park near to the M55, but the legacy stands.

Most of the larger hotels were taken over by these departments and thousands of civil servants were based in the area during the conflict. Arguably, the most important Government paper of modern Britain was written in the bedsits of the resort. The Beveridge Report, which would outline a new, fairer Britain with provisions of care from the cradle to the grave, was possible thanks to the room capacity of the resort and the town's ability to accommodate. The brainchild of the social economist William Beveridge, the finer details were hammered out in hotels and rooms up and down the resort. In the beginning, around 1,700 civil servants moved to the resort, with more to follow, mostly coming from the capital. Most of the large seafront hotels were requisitioned for government departments, in total nearly 50 were handed over to the civil servants. Small bed and breakfasts were also used by the various welfare departments with them taking residence in over 300 in the town alone. As well as moving to Blackpool, they also took over some of St Anne's bigger seafront hotels.

One of the departments that moved was the Department of Pensions, which took over the large Norbreck Hotel and stayed in the resort until well after the war. Along with the Ministry of Health, they also commandeered the historic and sizeable Rossall School in Fleetwood as a headquarters, the children being relocated to Cumbria. They briefly used the Cleveleys Hydro before relocating to green space in Norcross where they would remain for many years. Moorland Road, which also used to be a main employment base, was built during the war with many 'temporary' buildings being erected to house the staff numbers though they must have been built to last after all as they still house staff today. Other hotels that accommodated relocating departments included the Fernlea Hotel in St Anne's, which housed some staff from the Department of Food, and the Grand Hotel on Station Road, Blackpool which housed a range of civil servant activities. The large Imperial Hotel, famous in recent years for accommodating prime ministers during party conferences held in the resort, housed offices for both the Inland Revenue and the Ministry of Agriculture and Fisheries. This latter department was particularly busy in trying to boost productivity to feed the population. The department's Indian stores were moved to the Queens Hotel giving the area an international feel as the department hired many Indian workers too. The Northcliffe Hotel was used by the Ministry of Planning and Works, which was busy granting permission to rebuild demolished structures.

Blackpool played a part in the socialist welfare movement when it hosted the critical Labour conference in which the leaders chose not to enter into a post-war coalition government. This decision proved to be right for the party as Clement Atlee won convincingly, and they were able to implement full welfare provisions and Labour arguably had its finest hour. The Beveridge Report was published in 1948 and would not have been possible if it was not for Blackpool. The terms were groundbreaking and ambitious, and included support for the nation and the Fylde's most needy along with returning heroes. The Fylde's open-door policy to government departments would be rewarded when it came to administering these new benefits. The area had an experienced workforce thanks to the war and found itself with many permanent jobs due to the introduction of these new benefits. The socialist

Cleveleys Hydro Hotel, which housed the Ministry of Health.

movement required large new departments and staff, and the resort got some of this trade, which helped to give the future job market some much needed diversity away from the tourist sector that would prove hugely beneficial for the area for many years to come.

This is a great example of how future employment in the resort and surrounding areas owes its origins to the conflict. Many people continue to work in such organisations, including the DWP but also BAE Systems at Warton, which provide well-paid jobs in the area thanks to the US Air Force's decision to choose it as an airbase. The large Springfields Fuels site at Salwick served as a small armaments factory during the conflict.

CHAPTER 8

WARTON AERODROME – 'THE WORLD'S GREATEST AIR DEPOT'

Situated near to the Fylde villages of Warton and Freckleton, the airfield was originally marshland next to the main 'Lytham' road adjacent to, and near the mouth of, the River Ribble.

Initially the area was earmarked to serve as a satellite site to RAF Squires Gate, similar to the role of Stanley Park aerodrome, with the only difference being that Warton didn't have an aviation history and was purpose built. The base was needed to provide Britain with all-important increased aviation capacity. The history of the site, which is still integral to the area, traces its roots, like many other major sites on the Fylde, to the Second World War. The base is now home to BAE Warton, one of the biggest employers on the Fylde Coast, and is used as a production site, but as a nod to its Second World War past, it is still used to test aircraft. It also has an operational CAA licence, and can handle all types and most sizes of aircraft. Until recently, it was home to the Lancashire Constabulary's police helicopter and regularly caters for VIPs, ranging from the Queen to George Clooney. The facility acts as a satellite site to the Salmesbury factory, situated on the other side of Preston, which was also used during the war.

The site opened in 1941, but thanks to international events, namely Pearl Harbour and America joining the war, it was given a new purpose. It was offered to the American USAAF (United States Army Air Force) by the British command. USAAF was to use the site, along with others around the country (including Burtonwood just outside Warrington), for maintenance purposes. They chose the site because it was out of the way and, crucially, close to the port of Liverpool where the majority of material and men from America arrived. The base was substantial and built almost from scratch on marshland near the River Ribble. The architect was a Mr Thomas, who was tasked with building the huge depot, made bigger to spread the precious aircraft out in order to protect them from an air attack. The site was hastily built as the Americans needed it quickly, and the whole project was overseen by Lord Beaverbrook. As well as checks and repairs, it was used to process new arrivals, often coming in convoys to Liverpool and also via the River Clyde ports in Scotland. The job was for everything to be checked, assembled and tested which were then sent to operational squadrons for use in a range of roles including providing planes for Bomber Command; it was an aircraft distribution centre of sorts.

The airfield was built with three long concrete runways, which could cater for larger planes. The site was a vast area that had nine hangars in total located in various places around the airfield. The control tower, which was staffed eventually by American personnel, was a two-storey brick structure and is still used by BAE Systems to this day. Initially the personnel were expected to sleep in tents next to the operational airfield, but this was not ideal, particularly as the location on marshland near to the mouth of the river meant it was often cold and wet and the tents were exposed to the elements. Proper accommodation blocks were erected in due course which could cater for over 15,000 people, giving an idea of the extent of the operation. The accommodation blocks no doubt improved the morale of the men, who were many hundreds of miles away from home and in unfamiliar surroundings. In many cases, it would have been the first time the men would have left their parents and America itself. As well as money, goods and their Hollywood image, they also brought problems; America's black soldiers were treated and housed differently at the base.

The site was well defended with pillboxes, anti-aircraft defences and anti-landing obstacles. The exposed Clifton marsh was booby-trapped to make it impossible to land gliders near to the relatively exposed base. Amphibious landing was also discouraged via dug-in defences. The main road between the site and Lytham was also well defended with the establishment of vehicle check-points. The road had numerous concrete barriers placed across it to stop any unauthorised attempts to land by enemy aircraft, and to hamper any tank advances towards the site. These measures highlight how important the site was and it had to be protected with numerous men solely dedicated to this task.

One of the most noticeable effects of the airfield for the nearby villages (in particular Freckleton and Warton) was the influx of American personnel to the area. The first Americans arrived during 1942 and their numbers grew significantly until the site's recruits outnumbered the local residential population, hence the nickname 'little America'. They certainly changed the village and brought some excitement with them, as they would regularly visit the local pubs. Many a local entrepreneur cashed in on the new visitors both legally and on the 'black market'. The troops were well paid (more so than their British counterparts), away from home and frivolous with it. Most of the locals treated the Americans well, particularly the local women who were intrigued by the men, although of course at times there was friction. The airfield brought problems with crashes and excess noise as the engine sheds eventually worked twenty-four hours a day. Some feared the site was painting a target on their backs and that it might draw the interest of the Luftwaffe, although this never came. The site was quite well hidden and its inception coincided with a decrease in the Luftwaffe's bombing power and many other large new targets being built all over the country. The 'My British Buddy' episode of *Dad's Army* springs to mind, however, most people were happy to do their bit for the war effort and welcomed the excitement and opportunities it brought with it.

Freckleton and Warton had been transformed from sleepy Fylde villages to a hive of international activity. Many satellite buildings were used in the nearby villages with a military hospital being set up and numerous storage units created. There was an anti-aircraft gunning position near to the airfield at Grange Farm and a large railway goods yard which served the site on a spur of the South Fylde line with substantial sidings (which no longer exist). The service personnel travelled further afield, most noticeably to Lytham where many arrived by rail and Kirkham, which had its own population of military visitors, mostly in the RAF. They also visited Preston, the attractions of Blackpool and, when they had leave, would often go to London for dances and entertainment with other Americans serving in Britain. With a cinema, theatre, an American Red Cross building along with many sports clubs and recreation buildings situated on the base there was quite a lot to do. Due to the size of the site, there were many famous visitors to the base, including Bing Crosby, boxer Joe Louis, Bob Hope and Glen Miller, who played one concert on the airfield itself and then played in Blackpool. As the operation grew (as it did steadily throughout the war) the base was referred to as 'Army Air Force Station 582' because referring to it as 'Warton' would risk giving the location away to listening Germans. Burtonwood got off the ground earlier than Warton and dealt with more planes initially, but Warton soon caught up. Being a repair and processing centre for the Americans, the airfields saw a range of different American aircraft. These included B-17s together with other large bombers and the site specialised in Mustang Fighters and B-24 Liberators, with other airfields specialising in different models.

The sheer scale of the site at Warton airfield was staggering and it was one of the busiest military locations in the area during the war. By 1944, there were over 10,000 people (mainly Americans) based at the site. It was on a visit to the site from Lt Gen. Doolittle that it got its nickname as 'The world's greatest air depot'. The nickname stuck and represented the base's sheer capacity serving as a critical part of the Allied war effort. Before D-Day the airfield had hundreds of planes being worked on at any one time by the men, at its height the complex was home to over 18,000 men.

As expected with a site of such size and number of flights, accidents were common. There were a few crashes and incidents in which the casualties were mainly military personnel. Planes quite regularly ditched into the river on their landing approaches, and debris is still occasionally found in the area to this day (particularly by the shifting Ribble sands). The worst incident by far was the Freckleton air disaster (*see* Chapter 9) and this time it was the locals, mainly children, who paid the ultimate price. In 1944, two aircraft collided in mid-air over the river, the Lytham lifeboat crew responded but all involved were already dead. Some mechanics based at the site were drafted into frontline service to replace infantry lost in the push on the Continent and many did not make it back. By the end of the war, over 6,000 engines had been tested and over 10,000 aircraft processed at the site, testament to the hard work of those stationed at the base. By 1945, the last of the Americans had gone home and the site was handed over to the RAF. It continued production and is still busy to this day under the operation of BAE Systems, although never to the same extent as those hectic war years.

CHAPTER 9

THE FRECKLETON AIR DISASTER

Undoubtedly, one of the Second World War's saddest incidents took place in the sleepy Fylde village of Freckleton, lying on the banks of the Ribble estuary and close to Warton airfield. The disaster claimed the lives of many innocent children and decimated the small village for years afterwards. The incident took place on 23 August 1944, when an American bomber crashed into the local primary school, a row of three houses and a popular snack bar. The total death toll was a catastrophic sixty-one, including thirty-eight children.

It is estimated that 10,000 Americans were living in the village at the time of the accident. The day started like any other as Charles de Gaulle was liberating Paris with the Free French Forces on the Continent, the busy Warton aerodrome was in full operational mode. The children attended Holy Trinity Primary School as normal and Miss Hall, aged 21, a new teacher and former pupil of the school along with Mrs Hume, who was one week away from retirement, took their classes as usual. The regular noise of the American aircraft buzzing overhead was heard. Nearby Mr and Mrs Whittle opened up their snack bar, affectionately known by service personnel as 'The Sad Sack', which catered mainly for the many servicemen in the village. Their daughter Pearl was with them helping out whilst on her holidays from Queen Mary School in Lytham.

The only difference on this normal Fylde morning was the adverse and strange weather conditions. With reported winds of up to 60mph, heavy rain and thunder, it was certainly a stormy day. In fact, water spouts (small water-based tornadoes) were reported in the nearby Ribble Estuary, and the adjacent seaside towns of Southport and Blackpool had reported localised flooding in the downpours. It was at this time that two B24 Liberator bombers belonging to the USAAF, one plane nicknamed 'Classy Chassis 2' and piloted by 1st Lt John Bloemendal, set off for a test flight. Test flights were common over the area with the base repairing and processing aeroplanes it was an essential task to ensure planes sent to combat were in good condition. Shortly after take off, and due to the adverse weather, the planes were recalled by the control tower at Warton. One aircraft landed safely but the second, piloted by Mr Bloemendal, contacted control to inform them he was aborting his landing. This was the last that was heard from him.

The plane, already flying low from its aborted landing and in severe weather conditions where visibility was poor, crashed into nearby Freckleton. The plane first hit a tree, damaging the right wing, then falling fuselage hit three nearby houses and the Whittle snack bar, killing all three members of the family, seven Americans, some RAF personnel and civilians, including James Silcock, a 15-year-old boy who had just popped into the café for a cup of tea. The main body of the aircraft crashed into the infant area of Holy Trinity Primary School killing the two teachers and many of the pupils. The children were all around 5 years old and some were evacuees from London who had moved to the village to escape bombing, devastating the families back in the war-ravaged capital. This was one of the worst wartime civilian disasters in the country and it weighed heavily upon the village for years to come.

Shortly after the crash, villagers and servicemen alike flocked to help. There were many heroes, including a local policeman and the school head-master, Mr F.A. Billington. Seven children and two teachers were eventually pulled from the rubble of the school, but unfortunately both teachers and four of the children died shortly afterwards due to the severity of their injuries. They tried in vain to rescue those in the rubble, but an estimated 2,700 gallons of aviation fuel fell from the plane and ignited – it was a hopeless task. Some of those trying to help received severe burns as they tried to free people trapped under the collapsed buildings. One clock in a nearby class-room had frozen at 10.47 a.m. Service personnel from the nearby Warton site rushed to the scene to see what they could do, large searchlights were set up and people searched the rubble through the night. The disaster caused utter devastation in the village. It was reported in the news but the location was classified, perhaps hampering the nation's ability to grieve. Some details of the disaster remained classified even after the war, but the village knew what had happened that terrible day.

Bing Crosby visited the survivors in hospital after the crash and it is thought that he broke down in tears at the bedside of a bandaged young girl. He also sang some of his classics for the children. There was no hostility between the villagers and workers, they knew that accidents were inevitable, but the disaster took everyone by surprise. The villagers and the Americans had a good relationship and at many local events, such as open days, these recruits donated gifts for the local children, which helped to cement relationships.

The exact cause of the crash is unknown, but it was in all probability down to the weather. Structural failure due to adverse conditions was not ruled out and one eyewitness reported seeing the plane hit by lightning in the storm. A formal inquest took place on 8 September 1944, which criticised some of the American pilots for their belief that British storms were just 'small showers'. It recommended that all US aircrew be trained in recognising and respecting the dangers of British weather in an attempt to prevent a similar disaster happening in the future.

A 10ft-high gothic-style memorial cross stands in Freckleton churchyard as a permanent reminder of the disaster and the impact it had on the village. Shortly after the disaster, the Americans raised money for a memorial garden and children's playground. A plaque in the garden reads, 'This playground presented to the children of Freckleton by their neighbours of base air depot no 2 USAAF in recognition and remembrance of their common loss in the disaster of August 23rd 1944.' The opening of the playground was attended by some 2,000 personnel from Warton who wanted to pay their last respects.

The village still remembers what happened and, in 1977, the Memorial Hall was opened in the village. The original school no longer exists and houses were built on the site, but a marker placed there in 2007 serves as a permanent reminder of the terrible tragedy that occurred that summer's day.

CHAPTER 10

TIME TEAM AND THE WARTON CRASH

In an episode entitled 'The Bombers in the Marsh', Channel 4's *Time Team* visited the area trying to find the remains of two planes that collided after setting off from Warton airbase. The team, working with members of the Lancashire Aircraft Investigation Team, set out digging in an attempt to piece together the mystery surrounding the accident. The mid-air collision happened on 29 November 1944 when two A-26 Invader aircraft, with a combined crew of three, hit each other after setting off for a return flight to France. The A-26 Invader, made in America by the Douglas Aircraft Company, was a fair-sized bomber capable of carrying 1,800kg of bombs, which operated towards the end of the war. At the time of the crash, these particular aircraft had only very recently gone into service and the first had only arrived at Warton in September 1944. Pilots had very little experience flying them. As with many new planes, glitches were found, and one of the main drawbacks was the view from the cockpit, which was very limited particularly being hindered by the position of the engines on either side. Another major issue was that the aircraft required different operating techniques to other bombers, which were relatively unfamiliar to the pilots.

The planes took off around midday for possible deployment to the ongoing Battle of the Bulge counter offensive. The two American Air Corps pilots were 2nd Lt Kenneth Hubbard and 2nd Lt Norman Zuber, and the third crew member was Pte John Guy. The collision happened near to the base and towards the river in between Lytham and Warton. Many at the base looked on in horror as the crash unfolded. Eyewitness reports at the time describe a collision with one of the planes immediately catching fire, followed by a large explosion. The second plane crashed on the ground and had a large section of its wing missing. In fact, the engines from both planes broke away on impact and were scattered across the area. Other planes that were flying in the formation had to avoid being caught up in the collision. Both planes hit the ground in the marshy area alongside the River Ribble. Sadly, all three crew members died.

The 2005 *Time Team* dig was reportedly a difficult undertaking and a previous attempt to uncover the wreckage in the 1980s had failed. The marshland is almost inaccessible and the exposed nature of the estuary leads to unpredictable weather conditions. The investigators had to use special all-terrain vehicles just to get to the location and lead to Tony Robinson remarking, 'it's a bit like archaeology on the moon'. The information about the crash is limited and unreliable – the only evidence pointing to the location is a tail fin that could still be seen sticking up out of the ground, and sightings of a propeller in the area, all of which is now covered by the silt from the river. Television archaeologists, local volunteers and members of the investigation team dug a number of trenches using the nearby BAE site (standing on the original USAAF aerodrome site) as a base. They wanted to investigate what had actually caused the crash because the various reports were conflicting, as was often the case in a busy, potentially censored war environment.

The dig was quite successful as they managed to raise one of the engines out of the mud with its propeller intact and in relatively good condition, allowing the team to identify which plane it came from by using its serial numbers. On day two of the three-day dig, the team managed to locate and unearth the main part of one plane, with its cockpit becoming visible, by using geophysical methods. Also uncovered was a well-preserved and almost complete Browning gun, which had to be taken away by the bomb disposal team to be made safe. It turned out to be one of the largest digs performed by the television programme. Time constraints meant that they were unable to raise the second plane, although local teams did do some further excavations.

It was concluded that Hubbard's plane was hit on its undercarriage by Zuber's bomber as the result of a visual blindspot. Hubbard's fuselage had suffered substantial damage when it was hit from below by the propeller of the second bomber causing severe damage whilst still in the air, and the impact caused the planes to catch fire.

Despite it being a somewhat hopeless situation, the public attempted to help the pilots and Pte John Guy. The local lifeboat was deployed, taking on unfavourable conditions in a simple rowing boat close to the flaming wreckage.

Sergeant Stanley Begonsky was present and talked about his experience in a book documenting the US 8th Air Force shortly after the war. He told how he made his way across the boggy marsh before swimming to the wreckage in a tough current. Upon reaching the first plane he realised that the trapped men were already dead and so continued on, swimming among the wreckage of the second plane, with exploding ammunition adding to the danger. He managed to drag one body from the wreckage before he caught fire. It was too late and the damage too severe for his rescue attempts to be successful, but he later helped the lifeboat men gain access to the wreckage to retrieve the bodies for a burial. He was awarded the Soldier's Medal for his actions that day and crew from the lifeboat received awards for gallantry.

Parts excavated at the *Time Team* dig were taken to HMP Haverigg in Cumbria where the inmates helped to restore them prior to being placed on display at the museum at RAF Millom. There were numerous finds including small parts, a compass and a fully restored engine maker's plate containing detailed information about the plane it came from.

The crash changed the way in which the bombers were allowed to fly in formation and they worked on the visibility issues. No further A-26 collisions were reported during its service life, which continued well into the Cold War. The crash was ruled to be due to poor weather conditions and neither pilot was considered responsible.

CHAPTER 11

BOMBING RAIDS ON THE FYLDE

One of Axis Commands main objectives, particularly in the earlier bombing stages, was to undermine civilian morale by directly targeting the population. Blackpool, a large town in its own right, swelled to significant numbers during the summer months and bombs during this peak would have claimed the lives of people from all over the country. The propaganda impact of a direct hit on the resort, the playground of the nation and internationally recognisable, shouldn't have been underestimated. The real reason Blackpool was lucky however, was the sheer level of contribution that the town made to the general war effort itself. Certain aspects of the main national operation of conducting a sustained conflict could have been seriously hampered by a well-planned raid on the resort. The fact that the majority of RAF personnel were trained at the resort meant that a raid could have slowed down the ability for Fighter and Bomber commands to bring new pilots into operational units. Large numbers of soldiers took leave in the resort and there was an increase in the wartime population – the casualties could have been substantial.

There were other obvious targets from the air including four airfields, training ranges and other military targets. The huge Vickers factory that produced thousands of Wellington bombers would have also been an obvious target as a site of national production importance. A lone bomber targeted the factory, but missed and hit nearby Lindale Gardens. This would have been an opportunist target but the intelligence gathered from the pilot would have been relayed back to command as details of all raid activity were recorded at base.

German-made aerial reconnaissance maps were produced relating to the area with some specific locations identified, including the piers and tower.

Operationally Blackpool would have been a risky place to bomb because of the location in the north west of the country, which would have meant additional fighter support was virtually impossible. Blackpool did have air defences although they were light compared to large cities, and would have found it very hard to defend itself against a substantial aerial attack, as the defences were not in place. One could suppose that the Germans were unaware of the full extent of the strategic importance of Blackpool or it may simply be that Hitler's 'people's playground' was supposed to be left unscathed.

Although Blackpool was left relatively alone, it did not escape completely and bombs, although in relatively small numbers and unplanned, did hit Blackpool and the surrounding areas. Poulton-Le-Fylde, Kirkham and St Anne's also saw the wrong end of German bombs. The estimates released after the war are that 139 high-explosive bombs and over 1,100 incendiary devices hit Blackpool and the Fylde Coast. Of these raids, three resulted in a loss of life, with the largest loss occurring in September 1940 when Blackpool North Station was targeted. The bomber dropped around ten high explosive bombs around the station, after flying low towards the building. The station received only minor damage as, thankfully, the weapons were not very precise at the time. One bomb, however, fell into a nearby street and hit residential terraces. This resulted in eight deaths, the most from a German bomb in the area during the conflict, and fourteen people were left injured, along with substantial structural damage to the area. The bomb hit Seed Street and most of the houses were never rebuilt. Some of the dead had only just returned from a night out. The attack happened around 11 p.m., and seems to have resulted from a plane following either a train or the gleam of the tracks into the station area. It was quite common for pilots to follow railway tracks and canals, releasing the bombs when a terminus became visible. Eyewitness reports state that the bomber flew low, coming in from the north east, which is the direction in which the track makes it way to Poulton-Le-Fylde. It is likely that the pilot lost his bearing whilst looking for a larger target nearby. The raid was well remembered in the resort. One of the buildings hit was ironically the local ATC building (they also had a depot off Whitegate Drive near to the Saddle pub) which had taken up residence in a garage on nearby Buchanan Street, luckily the men were out dealing with other local incidents.

The raids in Kirkham and St Anne's were almost certainly opportunist targets for lost German bombers. In St Anne's a lone bomb hit, falling on several houses in Church Street in the Ansdell area. One person lost their life in the raid, which occurred on 1 October 1940, and nine people were injured. The Kirkham raid occurred in autumn 1941 and hit a large area, making a substantial impact with over 130 houses reporting damage. The direct hit also claimed two lives, injuring seven others.

Bombs hit South Shore, near to the airport, Leopold Grove (situated near the busy town centre) and North Shore golf club but without a loss of life. One bomb at the club failed to explode, possibly down to underground sabotage, and had to be dealt with by a bomb disposal unit afterwards. Fleetwood suffered a couple of hits with only minor damage reported with one falling between Fleetwood Road and Broadway. The crater now forms one of the ponds on Parr's Farm near to Fleetwood College Nautical Campus. A house in the Westbourne Road area of the town, near to Rossall School, suffered some damage after a bomb hit, allegedly after a raid on the nearby Barrow shipyards. The port of Fleetwood was hit by two bombs that didn't cause any major damage but served as a warning. Marton was also hit by a raid when incendiary bombs were dropped in 1940, with some hitting the town's gas works.

A raid hit Poulton-Le-Fylde in May 1940 and could have been a lot worse. It caused very little structural damage and there were no casualties, but it could have been devastating. The town was targeted by incendiary bombs, possibly dropped by path-finding aircraft to identify a target for a follow-up raid. Over 500 hit the area and caused some minor fire damage, however, had a bombing formation noticed the fire in the sky, made more noticeable by light restrictions enforced by the ARP, and acted the town could have been devastated. Targeting the town could have been a mistake but other bombers may well have followed as they did in other similar circumstances across Europe. The speed at which the volunteers worked to put out the fire may well have saved the town.

Being a seaside location, as well as bombs occasionally other dangerous things were washed up on the beach. Sea mines hit the town twice over the war period after becoming dislodged from minefields in the Irish Sea, which were laid to protect the coast. The first exploded in the sea off Gynn Square causing minor damage in 1941. The second went off near to the town centre. It was precariously close to the long promenade on North Pier. This occurred in 1943, but by luck, it happened out of season in a cold January so the area was relatively quiet. The blast caused quite a lot of damage and many windows were blown out in the town centre, but fortunately, no one was injured. It is likely that the mine was actually set off deliberately; typically done by simply firing at the mine thereby controlling the explosion and preventing more serious damage or loss of life.

CHAPTER 12

BLACKPOOL CENTRAL RAILWAY DISASTER

Just as Blackpool was getting used to life at war, it was hit with the largest loss of life in one event that the town witnessed during the conflict. It was a cold summer's day on 27 August 1941, tourists flocked to the seafront and the familiar sound of aircraft engines could be heard overhead. A Blackburn Botha L6509 training aircraft and four of 256 Squadron's Boulton Paul Defiant N1745 fighter planes took off from Squires Gate airfield on a routine training exercise when disaster struck. Flying near to the tower, the fighters dropped off, one by one, into a fighting formation – dipping their wings as standard. Three completed the move but the last crashed into the Botha that was flying at a lower altitude, hitting the plane in its midriff. Accounts of the accident were contradicting, but what is certain is that the fighter did not see the Botha underneath. The Botha was split in two and the Defiant lost its wing on the side of the collision. The horrific scenes, which unfolded around 3 p.m., were witnessed by tens of thousands of visitors taking advantage of a well-earned rest from war work in nearby areas.

The situation was made worse by debris falling from the planes and hitting the nearby town centre area. The Botha's fuselage crashed directly into the entrance hall of the busy Blackpool Central Railway Station. A chaotic scene followed, the whole area was covered in aviation fuel that inevitably caught fire and many people died in the most horrific of circumstances. The ensuing plume of smoke could be seen for miles and many onlookers flocked to watch the scene unfold, which sadly hampered the rescue attempts. One eyewitness, Percy Featherstone, who was 8 years old at the time, later recalled the horrific scenes:

I can remember my mother protecting me from the flames with a large jacket … my father picked up an injured baby from a pram. I lost the skin on the back of my hands, my trousers and legs were burnt.

People ran from the station entrance into the street with their clothes on fire and others were covered in burning aviation fuel. Percy was fortunate to survive but the death toll eventually reached eighteen, with thirteen dying at the time of the incident and five dying later in hospital. A further thirty-nine were injured. Owing to the popularity of the area for training, Blackpool suffered numerous aviation accidents.

Debris fell all over the south of the town centre, in areas such as Albert Road, South King Street and around Central Drive. The tail section of the Botha fell into the sea missing the busy promenade by inches, thus staving off further loss of life. The engine, however, scored a direct hit onto No. 97 Reads Avenue. The couple living there miraculously survived, although their home did not. The crew fell into the sea and the Blackpool lifeboat was deployed in rough seas and brought one body back to shore for burial.

The two military personnel flying the planes and one passenger on board the Botha died, the rest of the casualties occurred at the station. Many casualties were treated in the immediate aftermath at chemists and other local buildings before being transferred to Victoria Hospital. Among those that died in hospital was a toddler who was struck in his pram by debris from the falling aircraft. As well as civilians, some station staff lost their lives in the incident. Of the people who died, only one lived locally – a female resident and leader of the Blackpool Girls Club. The victims were from all over the country, such is the nature of a tourist town.

The mayor of Blackpool and other local figures visited some of the twenty-seven people that were hospitalised. The Air Minister, Archibald Sinclair, said of the incident in a telegram to the mayor:

I have heard with deep regret of the very sad accident at Blackpool yesterday in which an RAF aircraft crashed on the Central Station killing and injuring a number of people. Please convey to the relatives of those who lost their lives my deepest sympathy and to those who are injured my sincere wish for a speedy recovery.

An inquest was opened and a number of different witness testimonies given, but no blame was apportioned. Thanks to the large number of witnesses, the documentation of the incident was good and many people were called upon to talk at the inquest. Strict censorship of the incident meant that the location was kept out of the press.

The town worked to rebuild itself in the aftermath. Today the Coral Island amusement arcade lies on the site of the entrance hall to the old station. The house destroyed on Reads Avenue was never rebuilt and the Blackpool and the Fylde College Palatine Campus is now situated on the site.

Many heroic acts were reported in the aftermath. Five soldiers were given bravery awards: two were the soldiers who braved the rough sea to try to save the pilot. Others trawled through the wreckage and flames at great risk to themselves in a bid to save people trapped in the rubble. Among the civilians recognised was a member of the LMS Railway Police Force named Thomas Beeston, who braved the intense flames and saved the life of a young girl. The incident is one of the worst disasters in the town's history.

A plaque stands in Blackpool North Station as a tribute to the memory of those lost, the bravery of the public and the risk that railway staff took when serving in times of conflict. The plaque reads:

In memory of those who died at Blackpool Central Station on August 27 1941 and the brave efforts of PC Thomas Beeston (LMS Railway Police), Public Citizens and Rescue Services who did all they could to save lives.

Another accompanying plaque at the station reads:

To the memory of all the railwaymen and women of Blackpool who did not count the cost in times of conflict.

CHAPTER 13

RNAS INSKIP

RNAS Inskip, also known as HMS Nightjar, was an airfield operating during the war as a base for the Fleet Air Arm. As a branch of the navy, the airfields are traditionally given an 'HMS' name, similar to a vessel, in this case named after a bird. It was situated next to the villages of Inskip and Elswick, just outside Kirkham. The location was initially chosen due to its position near to the quiet coastline. Areas such as Pilling Sands and Morecambe Bay were ideal for training exercises and deemed sufficiently out of the range of enemy fighters. As with most of the Fylde area, it was flat, available and good for airfields. It was originally farmland and purchased from Lord Derby, Edward Stanley, a prominent Lancashire landowner who was awarded the Military Cross for his role in the Second World War.

The location was initially used for training, although it was chosen as an early radar station site after a somewhat unsuccessful attempt to utilise Blackpool Tower. Initially, the purpose of the base was to train crews on the techniques of taking off and landing on aircraft carriers. Another specialist area tutored at the site was anti-submarine warfare techniques, which were desperately needed to reduce the impact of U-boats operating particularly in the nearby Atlantic. Mock ship decks were built on the airfield, and the skills were taught and then re-taught to ensure the effectiveness of the training. Aircraft carriers played an important role throughout the war, reaching their operational peak in the Pacific Campaign against well-equipped Japanese opposition, who themselves had a feared fleet. The site itself was around 600 acres with many other local buildings requisitioned as peripherals to the main field. It was taken over in the middle of the war, in 1942, and as well as Inskip it also had a big impact on Elswick, which experienced a doubling of population during its operation, in fact, in the initial days locals referred to the site simply as 'Elswick'.

Some of the buildings in the area directly associated with the site are as follows: Shorrock's Farm; Catforth, which was used as a high frequency direction finding site; Thistleton Lodge, which was utilised as the medical quarters and a military hospital that was used by other operations in the area; Parrox Hall (in between Knott End and Preesall, Over Wyre), served as WRNS accommodation, even though it was some distance north from the site; The Prefect Hotel, 206 Queens Drive, Blackpool was also used as WRNS accommodation and Hingham Slip Inn Farm served as HQ for the site along with Inskip Lodge.

The airfield itself was built to a standard 'A' shaped runway design with two long runways crossing at the top. The site had a large number of hangars that could accommodate nearly 150 aircraft at any one time, and it was able to accommodate a large number of workers, often in quite poor living quarters particularly in the early stages of its existence. There were two camps for personnel stationed at the field with fourteen being expected to share a simple hut heated by a single stove. Many different naval aircraft used the site, including the Avro Anson and Gloucester Sea Gladiators. The most common aircraft to use the base was the popular Fairey Swordfish. The site was predominantly used for training although it did add other activities to its remit including fitting radar devices to operational aircraft visiting the base. Repairs were also completed with planes arriving direct from aircraft carriers. The site served a diverse range of purposes and was part of the bigger Fleet Air Arm operation during the conflict.

As with most big airfields, it suffered its fair share of accidents. Considered among the worst being when a Firefly crashed into the Irish Sea after take off – two people were killed. A plane also crashed into nearby fields shortly after taking off in 1943, narrowly missing the edge of Inskip and killing all of those on board the aircraft. The nearby Inskip church still houses a number of graves for personnel who died whilst serving at the base.

Local pubs such as the Derby Arms and the Eagle and Child saw a large increase in custom for personnel serving at the base. The rural pubs took some time to adapt to the livelier clientele. Many personnel ventured into Kirkham and Preston, walking the fair distance to Kirkham train station. Blackpool was a favourite with people at the site, who would take day trips to the Pleasure Beach during the day and finish by attending a dance at night. There were onsite recreations including sports facilities and the local cinema in Inskip held regular screenings and a weekly dance. Occasionally the venue housed some live acts, the most famous visit being from George Formby. Classes were put on in a wide range of recreational interests for the residents and everyone was kept up to date with news circulated in the onsite *Nightjar* magazine.

After the war, the site had a number of uses before the runways were eventually dug up. To this day, the site is a landmark; the four large aerials with their red lights at night can be seen for miles. The site is still run by the Royal Navy and is used as a communication centre, which opened in 1959 and specialises in low frequency submarine communications. It has acted as a listening centre, which was of particular importance during the Cold War and allegedly monitored Soviet submarines operating in the Atlantic. It is under the jurisdiction of the Specialist Naval Communications Agency. Recruits were known to travel from around the county to attend the site when it was used to hold Sea Cadet training. This closed in 2010 after nearly seventy years in operation. Training returned in 2012 and it is now home to an air-training and cadet centre for Lancashire and Cumbria. As the need for the runway became redundant, it was dug up and the concrete used for the back filling of the nearby M55, which opened in 1975.

CHAPTER 14

STANLEY PARK
AERODROME

The decision to open the Stanley Park Aerodrome was controversial, because Squires Gate already existed and people were unsure if the town could support two airports. Despite this, and thanks to the availability of cheap of land that was not present at the Squires Gate site, Blackpool Corporation decided to build the airport. It opened to flying as Blackpool Municipal Airport in 1928. The site covered roughly 400 acres and is now home to the zoo and De Vere Village Hotel and golf course. It was officially opened in 1931 to some fanfare with Labour Prime Minister Ramsay Macdonald officiating.

Although the airfield closed shortly after the end of the war there are still many clues as to the area's aviation past, these include a pillbox situated in Salisbury Woodland Gardens, built to protect the airfield and recently used to teach local schoolchildren from Stanley and St Kentigern's schools about the history of the site as well as conservation. More famously, today the airport hangars are used by the zoo to house the elephant enclosure. The old control tower is also incorporated into the zoo's main offices.

At the time of opening, the site was quite bare but as time progressed, and as many early aviation clubs used the site, more buildings were added including a clubhouse and hangars, which were built in 1931. One of the problems of the site was that it was too small with no real space for expansion and as planes got bigger, it fell out of favour. The runway was made from grass when the RAF preferred a more reliable surface, although wire mesh was added to it later on. It was quite a nice looking airport with some good Art Deco architecture, the curved hangar was the focal point and had

'Blackpool' lettered across the top. Despite the problems it did see some commercial success as an airport, particularly in the 1930s, as it provided flights to the Isle of Man, along with tourist flights catering for the resort's visitors. Due to the competition from Squires Gate, commercial flying had stopped before the outbreak of the Second World War.

Although it was far from perfect – it was the least important of the four Fylde airfields during the war – an already built airfield was too much of an opportunity to pass up. Thus, it took on what turned out to be the final task of its operational life – war work. The RAF took control in 1939 and the first thing they did was to sponsor a branch of the Civil Air Guard. The idea was to have pilots ready for combat if war broke out and it had nearly 250 members, headed by Stephen Williams. Also during 1939, in a show of strength to the Germans and reassurance exercise for the public, the airfield held an air show. Dubbed the 'Empire Air Day', the show featured a number of military aircraft including the state of the art Spitfires. After the outbreak of the war, the site was initially used for training, part of the larger RAF training scheme in the locality and specifically used for parachute training of new recruits. It also was used by the No. 3 School of Technical Training (Kirkham playing a big role in training mechanical pupils for the RAF later on) who were based on Talbot Road, Blackpool. Grounded aircraft were used by the school for training recruits. The main role during the war, however, was as a satellite site to the large Wellington factory situated at Squires Gate. Stanley Park was used as a secondary assembly line for the factory as output was increased. Five large Bellman hangars were built for the operation, favoured because they were portable and easily erected (taking approximately 500 working hours to build), which were placed next to existing buildings. These were just 5 out of 400 hangars erected in the early stages of the conflict. Bombers built at the site could only take off there, as they were too big to land on the small runways. As well as assembly for the Wellington bombers, the airfield was used as a repair station for planes damaged in the course of their duties. It specialised particularly in the Bristol Beau fighters, some being repaired by the Lancashire Aircraft Corporation. In 1943, No. 181 Gliding School used the airfield for training purposes; gliders were used nearing the end of the war, normally for troop transport and saw work in operations such as Market Garden in the Netherlands.

One of the last roles played by the airfield was scrapping some redundant Hawker Hurricane aircraft made famous as the staple aircraft of the Battle of Britain. Forty Hurricanes were scrapped at Stanley Park and it is said that souvenirs from these still exist in the local area.

One of the first airshows in Britain (c. 1910).

The site is often remembered for its famous female visitors, namely Amy Johnson, who regularly visited the site as her sister lived just north of the airfield on Newton Drive and Amelia Earhart, who alighted from a plane shortly after landing in Ireland to complete her crossing of the Atlantic and where she changed for London.

After the war, planes did not fly from the site again and it was originally taken over by the council as a storage site for illuminations and deck chairs. It was then taken over as the site of the Royal Lancashire Show before being transferred to the zoo after Blackpool Tower Zoo closed. Before the zoo was built, there were a number of ideas for the site, the most sensational being to build a Formula 1 racetrack. It was also seriously considered for the site of Disneyland Europe, the plans being halted at the last minute because of protests from business owners and attractions on the promenade that feared a loss in trade, and the park was eventually built in Paris.

CHAPTER 15

LYTHAM ST ANNE'S AT WAR

The South Fylde also played a vital role during the war, although perhaps eclipsed by the larger Blackpool. As soon as war was declared, the South Fylde area began to respond. Like many areas on the Lancashire coast, it accepted refugees from the big cities. The children often came from Manchester and Merseyside and arrived on the railway line. Local teachers and volunteers allocated homes to the children. King Edward and Queen Mary schools welcomed pupils from Manchester, Runcorn and London. Many of the big hotels in St Anne's-on-Sea near to the pier on the front were requisitioned for the war effort. A new fire station was built on Hove Road to deal with the predicted bomb damage, and air-raid shelters together with ARP (Air Raid Precaution) posts were erected around the area.

The area took in many different relocated government departments looking to escape London. The Fernlea and Majestic hotels housed the Ministry of Agriculture and Food and were a hive of wartime activity as domestic food production was maximised. The nearby Glendower Hotel was used as a base for the Ministry of Home Security keeping an eye on any threats to national security and organising responses to air raids, which undoubtedly saved thousands of lives. The departments moved into the quiet town and brought an influx of many workers with them. Bizarrely, the Soviet Embassy also relocated here and employed hundreds of people in the town. The government of Sudan also took residency in the Oxford Hotel. All available rooms in the Fylde Coast area were converted from holiday accommodation to supply the many different relocated departments with much needed space and beds and could be considered national assets at the time of emergency. Civil servants moved into the large Moorland Road site with temporary huts being erected to house the staff, building the foundations for what would become long-term job opportunities for the area. A large military hospital also used this site to treat people injured during war. Another site that owed its existence to the conflict was the St Anne's-on-Sea radar station, situated at the back of the town and quite a landmark it was initially built as a rotor radar station when the country's defence capabilities needed to be improved. One of a chain of similar stations, it was opened by the Air Ministry in 1940 in order to identify the position and track the progress of enemy aircraft flying over the country. The results were then reported to a command centre. The station is now the site of an aircraft control system. Locals also raised money for the war effort in particular for the boat HMS *Queenborough*.

At Fairhaven Lake, a defence command centre was established and heavily defended. The area was considered a risk because it was a prime spot for troops to land, and many remnants of fortifications still surround the picturesque lake, one is even concealed in a rockery wall. The famous sand dunes on Clifton Drive were not as serene as they are now as they were often closed off and used as a rifle practice range. Just across the road in what is now Lytham St Anne's nature reserve, anti-aircraft guns protecting the airfield were manned. The airfield brought a lot of air traffic to the northern part of the town and the skies were busy with the numerous aircraft from various airfields in the area. Not all planes were welcome and bombs were dropped on the area during isolated incidents. Many people were employed in the area, including those working at the Vickers factory in Squires Gate who found they often had to cycle on back roads to avoid raids and make it home safely.

The small port at Lytham was transferred over to war work and Operation Phoenix, the name given to the project to build 'Mulberry' harbours to support landing craft at the D-Day beachheads. They were used so that shipping and supplies could be offloaded and provided to advancing troops without the need for an existing harbour to have been captured. For example, Cherbourg took a long time to capture and then had to be repaired. Mulberry harbours were used to provide instant supplies to substantial armies in Northern France so they could keep progressing forward. The particular part Lytham played was to help build the reinforced concrete caissons, which were watertight and used to support the harbours, normally sunk into the ground. They were built at Lytham then transported to the south coast to be loaded for use once the beachheads had been secured. The location in which they were built was kept secret at the time, but is near the old docks. They were assembled in large sheds, which were next to railway tracks connected to the South Fylde branch line so they could be transported south quickly and easily. The docks also made other war products, including parts of landing craft.

The famous mid-eighteenth-century Lytham Hall belonging to the Clifton family situated close to the centre of the village was used as a military hospital during the Second World War. Its large size, numerous rooms and prominent gardens made it ideal for war work. The hospital was opened during a large ceremony by Councillor John Kay in October 1940 and was used primarily for treating convalescing soldiers.

Local Home Guard and ARP units helped observe the blackout and protect the town. In Lytham the Home Guard was called upon when a German pilot bailed out of his shot down Junkers fighter plane in 1941 after being hit by an RAF rival over the beach in front of the village green. He was captured quickly by the local units and held as a prisoner of war.

CHAPTER 16

HMS *PENELOPE*

During the war, Blackpool adopted HMS *Penelope*. The ship, built in the mid-1930s in case war did break out, was a light cruiser. Built by Harland and Wolff in the famous Belfast shipyard, it was quite a formidable weapon with considerable fire power. Fitted with large naval guns, torpedo tubes and significant anti-aircraft gunning positions, it was an important vessel and at one point even carried an aircraft. The vessel was manned by a crew of around 500 who 'ran the gauntlet' in many sticky situations. Local residents held a very successful fundraising event in 1941 during 'Warship Savings Week' and were able to adopt the ship. From then on, interest never wavered and the local papers gave regular updates on the vessel's escapades, bringing the story of the seas to the Fylde public. Many locals regularly sent food, gifts and letters to the crew and the relationship was cemented. The ship served mainly in the dangerous waters of the Mediterranean in which both Allied and Axis ships fought for control of the strategic sea and its ports.

Two of the most important locations in the area were the ports of Gibraltar and Malta. The *Penelope* guarded these vital convoys, which were the only hope of keeping the two besieged bases supplied and in Allied hands. The locals relied on the ship for food and the crew had to travel through extremely dangerous waters to carry out their objective. The ship also served other locations, helping to support the successful landings at Narvik in Norway. It was both a victim and perpetrator of attacks and gained a number of 'scalps' including numerous Italian ships attempting to supply the North African forces under Rommel. In the regions it served, largely under German air superiority, it was no surprise that the ship was regularly attacked. It was targeted numerous times in Malta alone, which led to the nickname 'HMS *Pepperpot*'. The constant attacks slowly took effect and the boat was docked for essential maintenance, even visiting the USA to be repaired. The crew spent their leave on shore experiencing the American hospitality.

Following repairs, the ship returned to the sea where it made its name under very different circumstances. The Germans had been driven out of North Africa, and Italy was in the process of surrendering, so the tide of the war was turning. The ship went to play a supportive role in the Allied advances. The ship, along with others, supported numerous Allied landings around Italy. Despite having run the gauntlet of enemy dominated areas in the earlier years and surviving many previous attacks, the vessel was sunk when en route to pick up ammunitions in Naples. HMS *Penelope* was engaged in supporting Allied landings at Anzio, Italy where the ultimate objective was to flank the entrenched German defences in the mountains around Monte Cassino and pave the way for the taking of Rome, ultimately hoping to shorten the war. The vessel encountered a U-Boat and suffered a direct torpedo hit, sinking the ship and killing around 400 men. The successful attack occurred as the *Penelope* was moving at high speed and some believe it to have been the fastest vessel sunk during the whole of the conflict. It was a clear indication that the war was not yet over. The report of the tragedy, as could be expected, became a 'bad news' story back in Lancashire, where locals grieved for the men who had fought on Blackpool's adopted ship. The legacy did not end there though as the famous author C.S. Forester wrote a book named *The Ship*, which was dedicated to the ill-fated HMS *Penelope*.

CHAPTER 17

FLEETWOOD
AT WAR

Fleetwood played its own unique role in the conflict not surprisingly revolving around its port and historic fishing industry. With Britain's safety lines threatened by Admiral Doenitz U-boat wolf packs and the need to keep Britain fed pressing, ports such as Fleetwood became increasingly important. Landing fish at the dock had a long history but the need for it during wartime was never eclipsed. The expertise of people in the town in landing and processing fish made the work highly important. Its role proved a vital lifeline for the country's food needs. In peacetime, the industry was fraught with danger and the town grew used to tragedy, but to fish in times of war reached new levels of danger. Along with the normal dangers of fishing, the presence of sea mines, enemy aircraft and enemy ships added to the pressure on the conflict.

As could be predicted, the Fleetwood fishing community suffered a series of notable sinkings. The merchant fleet did more than fish, with many of the town's boats being converted into minesweepers and experienced sailors from the town being deployed in various other roles in the community. As well as fishermen leaving the port others entered, including refugees who made Fleetwood their first port of call after escaping, often under intense conditions, occupied areas of the Continent. The town put them up, fed them and made them welcome and it was a place of safety. They were often looked after by the Royal British Legion. Other fisherman from places such as Iceland, the Faroe Islands and Denmark also landed at the port during the conflict and the town had an international flavour. Some stayed permanently but others simply unloaded their cargo at a safe port. The arriving foreign fisherman often had a lot of disposable income and were not made to adhere to the strict rationing in place, causing some unease with the residents. Like Blackpool, Fleetwood played a role in entertaining the troops and restoring some normality, even if it was shortlived. Many shows were put on in the town, which attracted visitors to stay in the area. Some of the larger hotels, especially on Queen's Terrace, were used as makeshift foreign consulates during the conflict, the area having only just recovered from an IRA bombing of the North Euston Hotel in mid-August, 1939.

Like many places in the local area, Fleetwood received its fair share of refugees from the big cities following the same protocol as most towns in the Fylde area. Whole schools moved to the resort for the initial period and Fleetwood Grammar School paired with a school from Widnes. Later in the war, the town also housed the No. 5 Medical Battalion with many American soldiers being housed in the port.

Fleetwood Port played a key role in the conflict and defences were built to protect it from enemy attack and sabotage. The approaches to the port and indeed the small number of arteries leading into the town were patrolled by troops and pillboxes were strategically positioned around the area. The port would have been vulnerable to attack, particularly from the air, and the Allied defence commanders recognised this. A large anti-aircraft position, which incorporated many guns, lay just over the river. It had a dual function, firstly to protect the vulnerable marsh and sands of inland Over Wyre and, secondly, to protect the Wyre openings and port channel approaches. What is now a quiet port was very busy during the war, with the channel to the sea via the river estuary hosting a hive of maritime traffic. More passengers were using the town's passenger ferry terminus because the majority of the Isle of Man services based in Liverpool were moved to Fleetwood due to the constant bombing around the Mersey. The port itself was probably the most defended point on the Fylde Coast and this gives us a clue as to the importance of the role it played. The town had other strategic places and roles to play but these in general were eclipsed by the need for the country's busy ports to remain productive. On the other side of the peninsula, there were also anti-aircraft guns and defences around the Esplanade and coast. Fleetwood Pier was also billeted with troops to stop the structure being used to land attacking forces and to keep an eye on the traffic coming into the port. Defenders feared enemy vessels such as U-boats attempting to halt the activity in the area and the waters near to the port were monitored by land, sea and air, with Coastal Command aircraft looking after the skies.

The significant number of boat losses from the town was a tragedy with many a modern-day family having suffered a loss due to the dangerous job. Fifty boats were lost during the war years, the largest rate of loss recorded in the port's history. Along with natural threats, such as running aground and bad weather, other threats tore through the fleets. Collisions were more common, particularly in convoys. The boats were constantly harassed by enemy aircraft and vessels; many damaged at the hands of U-boats. While the majority of the country waited until 1940 to see losses, Fleetwood had no rest period. The town lost its first boat, and the country its first merchant loss, days after the war began and this did not cease until hostilities ended. The boat, the *Davara*, was sunk on 13 September 1939 after being gunned down by a U-boat out at sea. More followed, notably the *Rudyard Kipling*, which was boarded by a German crew and destroyed. The seamen were treated well by their abductors who were the crew of the same U-boat that had sunk *Davara* only days before. Four vessels were sunk in one week during that September. In fact, the town's fleet had experienced losses associated with the Spanish Civil War as the bubbling cauldron of varying ideologies began to erupt. I have included a list of the boats associated with Fleetwood and lost in conflict below:

1939
Rudyard Kipling – destroyed by U-boat
Aurea – destroyed by enemy aircraft in the Firth of Forth
Thomas Hawkins – destroyed by U-boat
Delphine – destroyed by U-boat off the Irish Coast
Arlita – destroyed by U-boat
Davara – destroyed by U-boat
Lord Minto – destroyed by U-boat
Northern Rover – sunk
Creswell – destroyed by U-boat in the Shetland Isles
William Humphries – destroyed by U-boat in the Hebrides
Barbara Robinson – destroyed by U-boat in the Hebrides
Caldwe – destroyed by U-boat off the Faroe Isles
Sola – destroyed by enemy aircraft in the Firth of Forth
Trinity B – destroyed by enemy aircraft off Rattray Head
Sea Sweeper – destroyed by U-boat
Wigmore – destroyed by U-boat

1940

Victorian – destroyed by enemy aircraft in the North Sea

Lucida – destroyed by mine in the North Sea

Theresa Boyle – destroyed by enemy aircraft in the North Sea

Robert Bowen – destroyed by enemy aircraft in the North Sea

Cisnell – destroyed by U-boat off Fastnet

Hermia – destroyed by enemy aircraft in The Netherlands

Charles Boyes – destroyed by mine in the North Sea

Oona Hall – rammed by a French ship

Ocean Lassie – destroyed by a mine in the North Sea

Marsona – destroyed by mine in the North Sea

River Clyde – destroyed by mine in the North Sea

Hannah Reynolds – destroyed by enemy aircraft off the Dover Coast

Sea King – destroyed by mine in the North Sea

Velia – destroyed by mine in the North Sea

Joseph Button – destroyed by mine off the Aldeburgh Coast

Cremlyn – destroyed by mine off the Newcastle Coast

Loch Morar – destroyed by enemy aircraft in the Thames

Harry Hawke – destroyed by enemy aircraft in the Thames

Sea Ranger – destroyed by enemy aircraft off the Norfolk Coast

Ethel Taylor – destroyed by mine in the North Sea

Phyllis Rosalie – destroyed by mine in the Thames

Kenny More – destroyed by mine in the Thames

Loroone – destroyed by mine in the Humber

Margaret Rose – sunk at Dunkirk by Allied Forces to hamper future German operations

1941

Strathrye – destroyed by mine off the Great Orme

Robin – destroyed by mine

Fortuna – destroyed by enemy aircraft

Sylvia – destroyed by enemy aircraft in the Faroe Isles

Whitby – destroyed by enemy aircraft

Van Orley – destroyed in an explosion

D'Arcy Cooper – destroyed by enemy aircraft

Strathgairn – destroyed by a mine

Kiltkilinton – destroyed by enemy aircraft in the Orkneys

Evesham – destroyed by enemy aircraft in the North Sea

Cobbers – destroyed by enemy aircraft

Princess Louise – destroyed by enemy aircraft off the coast of Ireland

Kincorth – destroyed by mine off the Welsh Coast with 11 lost
Ladylove – destroyed by U-boat off the coast of Iceland
King Erik – destroyed by U-boat off the coast of Iceland
Thomas Deas – destroyed by mine with 14 lost
Force – destroyed by enemy aircraft in the North Sea
Craddock – destroyed by enemy aircraft off St Abbs Head

1942

Warland – destroyed by enemy aircraft in the North Sea
Botanic – destroyed by enemy aircraft in the North Sea
Ranonia – destroyed by U-boat off the coast of Iceland
Manor – sunk
Manx King – destroyed by enemy action in the Faroe Isles
Cloughton Wyke – destroyed by enemy aircraft in the North Sea
Irvana – destroyed by enemy aircraft in the North Sea
Braconbush – destroyed by mine
Caliph – destroyed by enemy aircraft
Northern Princess – sunk off the coast of Canada

1943

Red Gaunlet – lost to enemy attack in the North Sea

1944

Wyoming – destroyed by mine in the North Sea
English Rose – destroyed by mine off the coast of France
BraconBurn – destroyed by U-boat
Rochester – destroyed by mine
Noreen Mary – destroyed by U-boat

1945

Allenta – collided with a U-boat
Sweeper – destroyed by U-boat
Pinorah – destroyed by mine in the North Sea
Hayburn Wyke – destroyed by U-boat
Ethel Crawford – destroyed by mine
Daily Mirror – destroyed by mine
Arley – destroyed by mine in the North Sea

The vast number of ships sunk highlights the plight faced by the brave crews. The ships listed are all connected with Fleetwood with most setting off from the town. These are not all the ships lost during the period with many more lost due to more natural occurrences, those listed are the ones attributed to war, with a considerable amount being lost to mines. There was a large minefield positioned in the North Sea with many of the mines placed by the Allies themselves which caused the loss of many ships from the town. Germans also dropped parachute mines at strategic locations, such as river mouths. Many ships lost in the North Sea were used to complete the coal run from the Tyne/Tees to London via the dangerous Thames estuary. Some boats had near misses and the busy Fleetwood lifeboat was launched on numerous occasions to help stricken vessels. One such event happened in 1941 and related to a foreign schooner named the *Stella Marie*. The boat was grounded due to adverse weather conditions on the rocks near to the mouth of the River Wyre and the lifeboat was launched. The crew of the vessel panicked and many jumped overboard to try to swim to shore inadvertently positioning themselves between the large ship and jagged rocks. The lifeboat, guided by a Jeff Wright, positioned the boat to protect the crew and managed to save all the men despite incredibly unfavourable waves. He was awarded an RNLI silver medal for the skills he showed during the rescue.

Fishing at the port was also badly hit by these ship losses with smaller catches being landed as the losses worsened. Fleetwood did however process large amounts of fish from other fleets (from places like Lowestoft, Grimsby, Whitby etc.), who decided to land the catch in Fleetwood supposedly out of the way of the Germans. The number of ships lost decreased over time as the Allied Forces got the upper hand; anti-submarine measures had increased and air superiority transferred into the hands of the RAF. Not all of the incidents resulted in a loss of life, with some crew being picked up by other ships, but it was still a significant number for the relatively small population of Fleetwood. Even after the conflict ended, ships were still being lost to sea mines, because they became dettached from the fields. The town still remembers those lost and the Seaman's Mission organised many memorial services and gave support to the people most affected.

With all the losses the port shouldered, one vessel inextricably linked with the town was able to hit back. The vessel took the town's name and, rather aptly, was built to protect home waters and escort convoys. While the fishing boats were being sunk, HMS *Fleetwood* was doing the sinking of enemy vessels. The ship claimed two U-boat 'scalps', and, flying the flag for the town all around the world, evacuated soldiers from the early Norwegian Campaign before taking to its role perfectly as an escort ship to protect merchant convoys, their men and materials. Notable convoy deployments included Gibraltar, Derry/Londonderry and Atlantic convoy defences. The ship, unlike many similar vessels, survived the war and remained active until the 1950s.

A flotilla of boats departed from the port southwards as Britain needed all of its marine vessels. They departed for Northern France at great risk in order to save as many people as possible from the beaches of Dunkirk. The boats, such as *Dhoon, Edwina, Evelyn Rose* and the *Jacinta* (not the one currently on display as part of the Fleetwood Maritime Museum) were part of the wider effort which was a success as brave troops stayed behind and kept the Germans from reaching the shore. Thousands of men boarded any vessel they could to get back to Britain. The brave captains of the Fleetwood boats had to avoid constant air attack as the Germans at the time had superiority in the sky. The small town and its crews played a role in perhaps the most romantic operation of the war, seeing Britain snatching a victory from the jaws of defeat.

As well as bringing in goods and food, *Fleetwood* transported people too. People who were deemed a risk to the country were interned on the Isle of Man where a large part of the seafront was boarded off. These people often departed from the port after spending a night in Blackpool. Prisoners of war were also transported and allegedly had to run the gauntlet of the local children. The port business of John Robertson & Son, which made parts for boats, was put to war work. The factory produced specialist equipment for merchant and naval boats. As well as this, the factory converted trawlers into minesweepers for the war and many of these craft came from Fleetwood. A large section of the fleet (particularly the bigger boats) was allocated mine-clearance duties. The crews often moved with the boats and it was such a regular occurrence that a special dock was used by Fleetwood ships on the River Mersey.

Fleetwood largely escaped enemy bombing during the conflict although some bombs did land. A few houses suffered minor damage from, often stray, bombers and the port was hit a couple of times including a raid at the end of 1940, though no casualties are recorded. Enemy aircraft did buzz overhead and there were many alarms, a 'dog fight' involving two fighters took place right over the town before the aircraft drifted off towards a misty Morecambe Bay. The locals did everything they could and the town raised considerable amounts of money for the war effort. It also sacrificed the old ornamental cannons that used to stand aside the old wooden lifeboat house when people voted for them to be scrapped for the war effort.

CHAPTER 18

KIRKHAM
AT WAR

For an airfield to be successful, it needed all types of ancillary personnel. Out of all of the ground crew jobs, that of the mechanics, which was to maintain and repair the precious planes, was one of the most skilled and important on the field. Again, the Fylde was chosen as a place to train these men. The honour fell to Kirkham along with its neighbouring villages. In Kirkham, a large multi-trade training centre was built by the RAF (the site at the edge of Kirkham is where the prison stands today). The site was vast and all available space was utilised. Initially it covered 220 acres, but was situated on the outskirts of the town in order to allow further expansion as and when required. Construction, which was undertaken by George Wimpey, started in 1939 and the site opened in 1940. There were numerous buildings including accommodation blocks on the sites. Initially most of the personnel stayed in large huts that were not ideal for lengthy periods, but the more permanent buildings took time and materials, both of which Britain was running short of at that point. The trainees were expected to 'make do' and not moan as Britain was in its gravest hour.

Around 72,000 people were trained in Kirkham for the RAF. The site opened in 1940 and survived after the war, eventually closing in 1957 before becoming the prison. By 1941, the site was the main armaments training facility for the RAF. There were twenty-one different trades taught at the site and a whopping eighty-six different courses relating to weapons and equipment. Working on operational airfields was dangerous, particularly in 1941 when they were the frequent targets of enemy bombings. Working with numerous machines, fuels and tools, meant accidents were common. Many different specialist trades were involved, recruits could work on real equipment and the site was a hive of activity. Flight mechanics and flight rigging were the main trades taught and classes were taught by men with experience in aviation and mechanical fields, often by veterans of the Great War. The small town was soon visited by people from all over the Commonwealth coming to do their bit for the war effort. The site had the hangars and numerous different parts of aircraft on which to practise. Some of the hangars are in use today in the modern prison site, which occupies a somewhat smaller site than during the Second World War. The site even had a cinema where patriotic movies were shown to a willing audience. Due its size and nature, it had its own hospital wing that dealt with many small injuries, cuts and burns, as well as catering to long-term patients. A bomb disposal corps was also based at the camp.

Other sites sprung up nearby including a temporary accommodation site at Freckleton and the larger Weeton site. Weeton worked along similar lines being home to the No. 8 School of Training, opening on 21 May 1940 on the edge of the village on Singleton Road near to Lucas Flash woods. It also specialised in the RAF Driving School (the school also had offices on Warbreck Hill Road, Blackpool), which is now home to the Weeton army barracks. Recruits were often bussed in from Kirkham and again flooded into local hostelries such as the old Eagle and Child pub. It also taught conversion courses for flight mechanics in a similar way to its sister site in Kirkham itself.

Other specialist courses included a fire and rescue training unit and the No. 31 Bombing and Gunnery School. The site had instructional airframes set up for recruits to train on as well as classrooms and barracks. They taught a wide range of trades relating to maintenance and repair of RAF aircraft, as well as teaching woodwork and joinery skills for working with the wooden aircraft that were still in use at that time. The site also housed a military hospital, which was used by units from all over the area particularly the base at Warton. It is estimated that nearly 50,000 men were trained at the site and the legacy lives on with some recruits marrying local women. Parachute training and fabric repair sessions occurred at the site. Other more general programmes were blacksmithing, sheet metal work and specialist instrument making. As the war became more established, the RAF Police School moved to the site and these recruits were kept busy particularly on the Continent until well after the war ended.

As well as training recruits for the RAF, Kirkham had more than its fair share of prisoner of war camps and became the main place on the Fylde where prisoners were kept (although there is also reference to the old John Smiths Brewery on Central Drive housing prisoners during the war). Two camps were situated in and around the town, one near Newton with Scales and the other one close to Kirkham Grammar School. Lancashire was favoured for prisoner of war camps as it was considered safer to house prisoners in the north because the south and east coasts were at threat from invasion. The idea, particularly in 1940–41, was that if the invasion materialised the camps should not be at immediate risk and thus the captured soldiers could not be liberated and then turn against the defenders.

The camps were built as the Allies started to gain success and prisoners were flooding in. The site location may have taken into account the proximity to the camps at Kirkham, Weeton and Warton. The men at these nearby sites may well have been called upon should the need arise. The perceived threat levels presented by each prisoner were graded before arriving, with many of the highest category inmates (usually captured German officers) housed in Grizedale in the Lake District. Some were paraded at Deepdale, home of Preston North End Football Club, before being moved to local camps such as the ones around Kirkham.

The camp situated at Newton was for German workers and based just off the main road, which was possibly the site of a searchlight position used in the defence of Preston at the start of the war. As the bomber threat did not materialise the site was converted. The site consisted of makeshift buildings situated near to a wood. It possibly held Italian prisoner as well.

The Brockmill camp at Woodlands Hall, Kirkham, was situated around Moor Street/Ribble Road at the edge of the town. The site housed mainly low category Italian prisoners. Towards the end of the war, they were allowed out to do work in the local areas. There is a photo of Italian prisoners working on a Fylde farm and references to them helping at Millbanke (now a care centre) and the surrounding gardens.

As well as the permanent camps, the famous Kirkham windmill was used to house prisoners for a brief period over Christmas of 1944. The mill, a landmark in the town and reportedly the highest point on the Fylde, was chosen to house some German prisoners of war for an interim period. The prisoners were deemed high risk and were guarded closely. Guard duties were undertaken by soldiers based at the nearby Warton aerodrome. The prisoners' short stay passed without major incident.

Other sites around the town included a decoy site or 'starfish site' on nearby Clifton marsh. The site was deliberately made to look like a town and was built by local servicemen. The idea was to hamper German navigation and to attract bombs away from civilian/industrial targets and ultimately save lives and material. The idea of starfish sites did have some successes in areas such as Sheffield and Derby. The site used different lights, in particular flares, as it was intended to look like a bombed urban environment. The site was supposed to protect the port city of Preston from Luftwaffe bombs. The town was also home to the RAF tuberculosis hospital specialising in treating the condition, albeit quite rare, for military personnel.

Kirkham also occasionally fell victim to attack and one bombing raid in particular caused problems for the town, causing substantial damage to numerous buildings. The raid also cost lives and showed the population that they were not immune to attack. Although overshadowed by its bigger neighbours in Blackpool and Preston, Kirkham and the surrounding Fylde villages again played their part in the area's war effort. These efforts continued after the war as the Kirkham camp was used as a demob centre for troops returning from the Continent and further afield. The soldiers were paid, given a 'demob suit' and provided with assistance for life in wartime Britain, all in Kirkham. A war memorial stands in the town, which recognises the sacrifices locals made in the conflict. The memorial has twenty-nine names of soldiers killed or missing in action from the Second World War.

CHAPTER 19

THE BLACKPOOL COPPER AND THE 'GREAT ESCAPE'

This is the story of Frank Mackenna, the Blackpool police officer who was tasked with catching the people responsible for the massacre of the 'great escape' fugitives in post-war Germany, which was immortalised in the film starring Steve McQueen. The story behind the film was a mass escape of Allied prisoners of war from the Stalag Luft III camp in Silesia (situated in what is now Poland) in 1944. The prisoners, under the direction of Squadron Leader Roger Bushel of the RAF, decided that escape was necessary and an escape committee was formed. Bushel reportedly said:

> Everyone here in this room is living on borrowed time. By rights we should all be dead! The only reason that God allowed us this extra ration of life is so we can make life hell for the Hun ... In [the] North Compound we are concentrating our efforts on completing and escaping through one master tunnel. No private-enterprise tunnels allowed. Three bloody deep, bloody long tunnels will be dug - Tom, Dick, and Harry. One will succeed!

The plan was to build three tunnels, nicknamed 'Tom', 'Dick and 'Harry' in an attempt to tunnel under the camp and into the nearby woods where escape would be easier. The idea to build three tunnels was in the hope that one of them would succeed – if one was found they would simply concentrate on another. The camp, which housed a huge number of officers, was designed to make digging escape routes hard. Firstly, it was built on sandy soil not suited to tunnelling. Secondly, the camp huts were raised off the floor to make detection of digging activities easier and, thirdly, there were seismographs that could be used to detect any digging. Despite the difficulties, the digging continued and many an inventive idea was used in the design and execution of the tunnels. It was a massive undertaking with the tunnel needing 600 men in total to construct. The idea was that over 200 prisoners would escape – a huge break out and a massive undertaking as all were to be given papers and civilian clothing.

The first tunnel to be completed was the infamous 'Harry' tunnel. The escape idea was to split the men into two groups. The first group was comprised of people who had the best chance of escaping, namely German speaking or previous escapees, together with the people who had worked hardest on the tunnel. The second group (nicknamed 'Hard Arses') were given basic papers and were deemed to have little chance of success.

On 24 March 1944, a moonless night, the escape commenced but catastrophe struck when the first escapees realised the tunnel exited short of the woods and in full view of a German watchtower. Nevertheless, the escape commenced as it was deemed too late to turn back. Even with the problems, which included an Allied air raid in the area, seventy-six of the first group managed to escape and made it into the woods without being seen. This in itself was a great achievement, but a huge manhunt saw seventy-three recaptured. The three successful were all RAF pilots – two Norwegians managed to reach Sweden by boat and a Dutch pilot made the mammoth trip to neutral Spanish. Fifty of those recaptured were executed, including twenty-two British prisoners. All were unarmed and supposedly protected by the Geneva Convention. The news of the execution reached back to the devastated prisoners at the camp. The prisoners of Stalag Luft III were eventually liberated by advancing American troops in 1945.

Politicians in Britain demanded justice after an address at the Houses of Parliament by Home Secretary Anthony Eden regarding the incident. He was quoted saying:

> We will never cease in our efforts to collect the evidence to identify all those responsible and are firmly resolved that these foul criminals shall be tracked down to the last man, wherever they take refuge. When the war is over, they will be brought to exemplary justice.

Frank Mackenna was picked to lead the search of post-war Germany for the perpetrators of the massacre. Frank, originally born in Accrington, moved to Blackpool as a child with his family where he attended Sacred Heart School in the town. Mackenna and his brother both became detective sergeants with the Blackpool police force. Mackenna's passion for flying saw him joining the RAF after he was cleared from his reserved occupation when the losses of Bomber Command were high. He flew numerous Lancaster bombing sorties over occupied Europe. The combination of his RAF experience, detective work and a desire for justice made him the ideal candidate for the job as lead investigator. By 1945, having been promoted to Squadron Leader, he was transferred to RAF Special Investigation Branch, which was established to solve serious crimes relating to the airforce.

Around seventeen months after the massacre, 38-year-old Mackenna went to Germany with one ideal, to obtain justice for the men who had been killed. When arriving in Germany for the first time he had little information to go on. Most of the records of the event had been destroyed, mainly by Gestapo officers predicting a post-war crack down. The investigation was all the more difficult because Germany was still suffering the effects of war and the defeated nation was immersed in increasing political strife between Russia and the other allies. Mackenna did not speak German and had only one staff member – interpreter Warrant Officer Williams. It is likely that Mackenna's desire to capture the perpetrators was increased by the fact that he knew two of the men killed, Edgar Humphreys and Robert Stewart, whom he met at RAF Squires Gate where they had both been stationed. Frank was a regular visitor to the airfield throughout the war.

Despite the difficulties, he had his first lead, thanks somewhat surprisingly to the help of some German soldiers. Wilhelm von Lindeiner was appalled by the slaughter and informed Mackenna that all the victims had been secretly cremated and their ashes taken back to camp. With this small piece of information, Mackenna took to the local crematoriums in the hope of discovering more information.

During a drive in the German countryside, an attempt was made on the investigator's life. A metal wire was strewn across the road in the hope of decapitating him, but, fortunately, the attempt failed. This highlighted the dangers of working in a hostile territory at the time, particularly to members of the RAF.

After further hard work investigating and visiting many post-war prisons, Mackenna and his now larger team were starting to get results. With a list of wanted men, the team started making arrests. One arrest, perhaps the most famous, was of Emil Schultz who had been responsible for the murder of the escape leader, Roger Bushell. Even in the face of his enemy, Mackenna showed compassion and, contrary to procedures, took a final letter to Schultz from his wife. By the end of his stint, thirteen Gestapo officers had been sentenced to death for their part in the murders and many more were given prison sentences for their varying involvement.

Blackpool resident, Frank Mackenna played a vital role in bringing the perpetrators of these heinous crimes to justice. Mackenna received an OBE for his work with the RAF and he eventually returned to the town to work for the Blackpool police after a brief stint in Cyprus where he was mentioned in dispatches. Frank Mackenna died aged 87 on Valentine's Day 1994, finally putting an extraordinary life to rest.

CHAPTER 20

BLACKPOOL FC AT WAR

Blackpool FC played an important role in providing an escape from the wartime tension despite the league being suspended due to the threat of enemy action. Many players were in the armed forces so were unavailable to play for much of the war. Full back Johnny Crosland received a distinguished flying medal for his bravery serving as a Fleet Air Arm pilot in the Far East. The club ploughed on and captivated the locals throughout and after the conflict, providing a distraction from the reality of war.

Many Blackpool 'Seasiders' believe the team were denied their true chance at winning the football league for the first time because of the war. It is true that upon the suspension of the league, in 1939, Blackpool were top of Division One, undefeated after three games and had acquired the maximum points possible. All football matches were initially stopped completely as the Government deemed it too risky to have large crowds congregating in one spot, fearing the impact of enemy bombers. When the threat abated, football was allowed to continue, although in a new regional format. Many teams were struggling with the majority of their players commandeered for the war effort. Although the new system was supposed to allow play to continue, sometimes it was not possible. A ban on travel for players who were required to stay within the area of their garrison town hit Blackpool hard. It meant that on one occasion Blackpool had to pull out of an away game at Manchester City. Man City were sharing their ground at Maine Road with arch rivals Manchester United, as Old Trafford had suffered bomb damage due to its location near to the industrial area of

Match programme from 1943.

Trafford Park located in the west of the city – a good example of 'enemies' coming together in dire times. Blackpool found they could only field one first team player who was based in Manchester, and therefore took the decision to withdraw from the Cup, to avoid bringing embarrassment to the club and the competition as a whole.

If the club suffered in some respects, it also benefitted from the town's important place in the war, particularly in relation to the availability of skilled recruits from the local RAF bases. By far the most famous 'guest' was Stanley Matthews, who served in the resort training RAF recruits in fitness as a physical training instructor (taking advantage of his footballing and boxing background, his dad was known as the 'Boxing Barber of Hanley'). Being unable to make his way back to Stoke, he played eighty-seven games for Blackpool during the conflict as well as being a guest player for clubs in Scotland, playing games for Arsenal and Stoke City, and playing unofficial England internationals, one of which would get him into hot water. After the war, he chose to settle in the resort, eventually living on St Anne's Road near to Pedders Lane. Matthews Court (with one road sign somehow spelt incorrectly!), just off St Anne's Road, is a reminder of South Shore's famous resident. With Matthews having settled in the resort and wanting a move to a more competitive division, the war paved the way for Blackpool to retain its most famous player.

Matthews played well partnered with Stan Mortensen, but it was another player, Jock Dobbs, who was the star of Blackpool's wartime football being the top scorer on four occasions during the season. As it is widely commentated in footballing circles, the war robbed Matthews of his best playing years and the same could be said for the team in general. Blackpool had some success in the war leagues, and also possessed some of their best players and played good football. In 1940, Blackpool reached the quarter finals of the 'War Cup'. The club won the League War Cup (Northern Section) after beating Sheffield Wednesday and went on to win their greatest wartime achievement, the Challenge Cup, after beating a strong Arsenal team 4–2 at Stamford Bridge. They also topped one of the two wartime leagues in 1943 as well as reaching a second Northern Section Cup final, this time being beaten by Aston Villa.

As well as a lack of players, Blackpool had to 'make do and mend' on numerous occasions as textiles were short and rationed during the war. The club struggled with old equipment and kit until, in 1943, they received thousands of clothing coupons granted to football clubs enabling them to renew their supplies.

SNAPSHOTS OF THE PLAYERS — *continued*.

DODDS. Centre-forward. The one-time Sheffield United favourite. Joined Blackpool in 1939 and is cracking goals for them in wartime football, just as he did for United, who got him for a song from Huddersfield Town. One of football's £10,000 stars; a Scottish International. Has scored 44 goals for Blackpool this season. Like several other members of the team, is in the R.A.F.

FINAN. Inside right. A brilliant player, who has rendered the club yeoman service for several seasons. Dangerous anywhere near goal with both head and foot. Born at Old Kilpatrick.

BURBANKS. Outside left. Brilliant winger of Sunderland, whom he helped to win the F.A. Cup in 1937. Played for Doncaster in wartime football for a spell before being moved to the seaside. A native of Bentley, he played for Thorne Town and Denaby, who transferred him to Sunderland.

TEAMS FOR TO-DAY

SHEFFIELD WEDNESDAY
Colours : BLUE & WHITE VERTICAL STRIPES ; BLACK KNICKERS.

Right Wing   Left Wing

MORTON

2 ASHLEY   3 GADSBY

4 RUSSELL   5 MILLERSHIP   6 COCKROFT

7 REYNOLDS   8 ROBINSON   9 F. MELLING   10 THOMPSON   11 SWIFT

Referee : Mr. F. W. WORT (Liverpool).		Linesmen : Mr. H. BERRY (Huddersfield). (Blue & White Flag) Mr. W. MARTIN (Leeds). (Red & White Flag)

11 BURBANKS   10 FINAN   9 DODDS   8 DIX   7 GARDNER

6 JOHNSTON   5 HAYWARD   4 FARROW

3 HUBBICK   2 POPE

SAVAGE

Left Wing   Right Wing

BLACKPOOL
Colours : TANGERINE JERSEYS, WHITE KNICKERS.

"Story of the Football League"

Is still available at Pre-War Price of

10s. 6d. (plus Postage 9d.)

From

THE FOOTBALL LEAGUE OFFICES,

102, FISHERGATE,

PRESTON.

Match programme showing the team line-up from 8 May 1943.

The war had its pros and cons for Blackpool FC – they were denied the chance of legitimate club and league success, but they gained Stanley Matthews and Polish pilot Adam Wolanin, who later went on to represent his home country in a world cup, playing for the 'Tangerines'. Another of their great players, Jimmy Armfield, moved to the resort during the conflict, originally being moved out from Manchester (Denton) as a child to avoid the bombs. He went on to become a legend, even captaining the England team, with the South Stand at Bloomfield Road being named after him. He still lives in the resort near to the airport and has family living in the town. Financially, the club gained with the ground being frequently let out to the War Office for games, primarily between servicemen. It also played home to American Football to cater for the US soldiers in the area, much to the amusement of the footballing locals. The rent actually helped the club out of a sticky financial situation.

The sport offered a respite for many spectators and players alike who wanted to forget about the war. Bloomfield Road played a part in this and people, if they could get the time off work, flocked to the big games to forget about the wider situation. It was a place to forget about the Hun, the next week's work targets and the rationing. In this respect, it was invaluable for the local population. Football is considered a great leveller; consider the 'no man's land' match played during the First World War. In fact, in 1936, Blackpool hosted FC Wien, an Austrian team, who they managed to defeat in a close game. The secretary remarked, 'These footballers have come on an embassy of friendliness from their country to ours, recognising that our sport is the greatest peacemaker in the world.' The visitors were well received on the day as was the nature of the game.

The important role the club played as a centre of the community continued after the war. Attendances rose sharply as people just wanted to have fun after the dire years of the war. So much so that in 1946 the club had to implement an 'all ticket' system for the first time in its history for the Boxing Day visit of local rivals Blackburn Rovers. Over 25,000 attended, which is higher than today's team commands for the Premier League season. The club capitalised on this and money was made, which would help to lay the foundations for their most successful time as a football club and keep the players they needed in the squad. The ground was also improved as the attendances were increased. Initially, new crash barriers were brought in for crowd safety reasons, before expansion plans were put forward for consideration. The rationing continued for many years, indeed, in 1949, the club was refused a licence to sell sweets at half time.

CHAPTER 21

BLACKPOOL FOOTBALLERS' WARTIME WRONGDOING

Two of Blackpool Football Club's biggest names were caught up in a little wartime misbehaviour. Stanley Matthews and Stan Mortensen, who both have stands named after them at Bloomfield Road, were caught trying to sell contraband goods on the Continent during the conflict. Both players served in the RAF, Matthews worked as a physical training instructor taking new recruits on runs and drills throughout Blackpool as part of a wider RAF training programme and Mortensen, 18 years old at the outbreak of war, was a wireless operator who served in combat in the skies over Europe. In fact, on one occasion, his plane crashed and he was lucky to escape major injury. The incident occurred towards the end of the war and was a mark on their respective records.

Both were in their footballing heydays when they were called up for a Forces football team 'friendly' against a Belgian team. The idea was to boost morale and be a good propaganda exercise. The location was a war-torn Brussels; Belgium had suffered German occupation and was only recently liberated. The fanfare of liberation had finished and the clean up had begun. Mortensen had been drafted in due to his form and Matthews had in the past played on the Continent (he was even made to give a Nazi salute in a match against Germany in 1938 at the height of appeasement). The game was played in March 1945 with the British representatives winning against a local side whilst providing a much longed for distraction for the country's people.

The problem occurred when the two players entered a jewellery shop in Brussels to look at gifts. They looked at the stock and tried on a couple of bracelets. Mortensen then proceeded to open a large suitcase containing rare goods, the value of which was highly inflated particularly in a country that was ravaged by war. Footballers' wages were not the same then as they are today (Mortensen later ran a paper shop, trading on his name, situated on Central Drive in Blackpool) and the temptation must have been too much. They offered the woman that served them coffee and soap, both sold at a premium due to lack of supply, not knowing that they were being tracked by the RAF investigations branch.

Workers at the jewellery store later told investigators that they paid 250 francs for a kilo of coffee as well as 40 francs for ten bars of soap. Mortensen had even signed autographs for the staff members to keep as a memento.

Both were charged with 'conduct prejudice to good order and discipline' and their names were stained. With evidence mounting up, both admitted selling coffee and illegal goods, citing that they had used the goods in an exchange for jewellery for their wives and not for personal gain. They were given stern words of warning.

CHAPTER 22

SHORT STORIES

The Blackpool Stronghold –
A Chindit Position in Northern Burma

In 1944, the Chindits (a British Indian 'special force' operating behind
Japanese lines in the Far Eastern jungles during the Second World War) set up
a defensive position on the Mandalay railway line near a town in Northern
Burma called Hopin. This stronghold was called 'Blackpool'. The point of
this position was to intercept the Japanese communication lines in Northern
Burma, particularly the railway line and major road near to the Japanese lines.
The 111 brigade led by soldier and author John Masters, set up a block at the
Blackpool position and within days it had come under heavy attack from
Japanese forces as the position was close to the Japanese Northern Front.
The position withstood heavy attack for weeks including a sustained attack
on 17 May. Eventually, during another large attack on the 24 May, part of the
position was lost. Despite heroic attempts to protect the stronghold shortly
after the latter attack, due to a large monsoon and the fact the soldiers had
been fighting continuously for seventeen days, they abandoned the position.
Many people lost their lives including nineteen Chindit soldiers that were
too injured to move and were shot by medical orderlies rather than being
left to mercy of the Japanese attackers. It is unknown why the position was
called Blackpool.

Blackpool Sand

As you would expect with a large seaside resort, the sand was used for the war effort, particularly locally. The sand the resort is famous for was converted into sandbags for protecting public buildings and, ultimately, lives. Volunteers were used to fill the bags, mainly men from the local Home Guard units. It was a laborious job and very hard work particularly in a strong Irish Sea wind with the tide and time constraints. The volunteers were supervised as the bags they filled were made from precious imported material, normally jute, which, like many things, was at a premium price during the war. A small team was expected to fill a full bag per minute, as they were needed straightaway to protect civil buildings and military instalments throughout the coast. Sand is still commercially excavated from the Fylde Coast to this day at St-Anne's-On-Sea.

Wrea Green Pond

As North West soil is known for its high percentage of clay, many brickworks were set up in the county. The largest and most famous of these works was in Accrington, where the red bricks, which were used for building a lot of houses in the area, were produced. The Fylde was not an exception and a small brickworks was opened at Wrea Green, moving slightly inland to avoid too much sand content in the ground. Clay soil was excavated in commercial quantities from the centre of the village. In fact, the famous pond many people believe was created purely for aesthetic reasons was created and filled because of the excavation for the local brickworks. With the blitz and large amounts of damage, bricks were needed urgently all over the country and the brickworks at the village helped to meet this demand.

Blowing up Bridges

In the event of an invasion, the two Wyre bridges, at Cartford and Shard, were to be blown to pieces to hamper enemy advances on the Fylde Coast. Local defence plans show the strategy involved a last minute blowing up of the bridges by trained professionals. The action may well have cut off retreating locals and split up families, but the idea was to stop advancements, particularly of tanks and heavy machinery. The outcome of the demolition would have depended on where the invasion hit locally. For instance, it could have protected or trapped Over Wyre. The most likely invasion site would have been around the Morecambe Bay coast of Over Wyre and this demolition would have prevented an immediate flanking of Blackpool and the South Fylde and brought the inhabitants more time to defend or retreat inland further into Lancashire. This is a great example of how defenders thought strategically and how individual localities would be affected by military command decisions taken locally or nationally. Other Over Wyre sites were to be used if an invasion took place. For example, it is said that there were plans for the various salt mines to be used for hiding and for resistance movements.

Pilling also housed a huge fuel dump installed by the Americans towards the end of the war, which was protected and near to the large sea defences. The need for fuel was a critical one particularly when advancing large distances into Europe after D-Day and this site was one of many fuel dumps dotted around the country.

Building the Biggest Ammunitions Site in the World

The contract to build what was then the largest ammunitions factory in the world, the Royal Ordnance factory site at Buckshaw Village, just outside Leyland, was given to a Blackpool-based building contractor, Sir Lindsay Parkinson. His company had an office at the Talbot saw mills in Blackpool. They oversaw a substantial workforce of over 4,000 men, such was the scale of the site. There were huge building projects constructing the factory itself and supporting buildings. The location of the site was ideal, near large labour resources and in a secluded area as well as being situated near the west coast mainline. The construction was complicated and as a major requirement for an ammunitions factory is water, to obtain what they needed they tapped into a pipeline running from the Lake District to the Peak District. It is said that this pipeline can still be seen running next to the Chorley to Manchester railway line over ground. The building of the plant was kept secret due to its strategic importance. The contractors used significant amounts of concrete, much of it coming from around Chorley itself. The huge site was built with expertise and labour from Blackpool. When completed there were near to 1,500 buildings on the site alone.

Amy Johnson and Squires Gate Lane

Many people may believe that the road adjacent to Morrisons supermarket and Blackpool airport is named 'Amy Johnson Way' simply because of the connection of the area with flying. Johnson was in fact a regular visitor to RAF Squires Gate during the war and had connections with the resort itself, including a sister who lived near to Stanley Park (on Newton Drive). The pilot, made famous by her solo flight between Britain and Australia, actually, like many female pilots, served in the Air Transport Auxiliary (ATA) during the war. The primary job of the ATA was to pick up and deliver aeroplanes and she could frequently be seen flying over the Fylde. She died in service after setting off from Blackpool on a flight to RAF Kidlington in Oxfordshire. She ditched into the Thames Estuary and despite a rescue attempt that claimed an additional life she drowned. The death is still regarded as suspicious and many believe the subject of an official government cover up, with reports of clandestine activity taking place and an additional person being on board her plane – someone whose identity needed to be protected. There are also reports that she was in fact shot down by Allied forces for failing to comply with air procedure. It remains a mystery to this day.

Blackpool's First Volunteers

Some of the first volunteers from the resort were formed into the 137th Regiment (Blackpool) of the Royal Artillery. The regiment fought in the ill-fated defence of Singapore, at the time a Far Eastern empire possession. With the Japanese surrounding the island, the position was hopeless and the soldiers were ordered to surrender by the British command. Surrender was seen as dishonourable in the Japanese's Bushido code, and many of the prisoners were put to work in horrid conditions on the Burma railways, immortalised in films such as *The Bridge on the River Kwai*. Singapore fell on 10 February 1941 with 445 Blackpool men taken prisoner, leaving hundreds of worried locals waiting for news.

The Blackpool Tower at War

Initially, nearing the outbreak of the war, the tower was used as an early radar post in an attempt to defend Britain. In order for radar to be fitted to the tower, the RAF, who operated the site, removed the crow's nest structure to allow the building of the station. It was known locally as 'RAF Tower', but the structure proved unsuccessful and it was removed. A picture can be seen with a series of horizontal aerials sticking out from the tower at regular intervals. The top part of the tower itself was taken down and radar installations were placed on the very top. The 520ft structure was utilised for other reasons too as the panoramic view could be used as a viewing platform by the local constabulary and ARP during the war to ensure the blackout was being observed. Lord Haw-Haw even announced on enemy radio that the tower had been attacked by the Luftwaffe and collapsed into the sea as a propaganda trick. There have been reports that a replica tower was built on a hill in North Wales in an attempt to confuse the Luftwaffe and, in particular, their reconnaissance planes in their early stage mapping of the country by air, but a decoy has never been found and no evidence is available that one existed.

North Shore Golf Club

North Shore Golf Club was hit by enemy bombs, one of which left a huge crater, a photo of which with the tower in the background is one of the best photos taken of the resort during the conflict. The golf course was commandeered for war work and golf took a back seat. The large open spaces were converted into growing areas as the need for food overtook the need for leisure; food grown helped supplement local produce. Other parts of the course had a number of defence features installed and were used by the RAF. After the war ended, the course was reinstated for golf by Italian prisoners of war who completed many similar projects across Lancashire. The course was also used for training exercise such as bayonet runs. Other golf courses in the area were also turned over to livestock grazing as every piece of earth had to be productive for the population.

Death in the Air-Raid Shelter

Air-raid shelters were built to protect lives, but in a slightly odd turn, on 24 July 1944 the partly clothed body of 22-year-old Joan Long was found inside an air-raid shelter on the promenade, near to North Pier. Private Thomas Montoya of the USAAF was court-martialled in October 1944 in Blackpool for her murder, but instead was found guilty of her manslaughter by suffocation. He was given a ten-year sentence. The murder unnerved town and had some worried about the sudden influx of foreign soldiers. It caused a little bit of tension shortly afterwards although most appreciated it was an isolated incident.

Preesall Sands Practice Range

The vast marshy spaces of Preesall sands were utilised for the war effort as an aircraft bombing test range. The location was chosen thanks to its similarity to other European landscapes, its variety of geological features and its location (deemed far enough away from the eyes of the Luftwaffe). The site was mainly used by the Fleet Air Arm for bombing practise. It shared a special relationship with HMS Nightjar with many of the planes that practised on the range setting off from there. Numerous targets were set up for practise bombing and included a full replica steel aircraft as well as smaller targets representing submarines (including a brick-built U-boat) and their periscopes. The idea was to train crews for operations involving both bombing coastal targets on the Continent and for anti-U-boat duties in the Atlantic. The test range was tough for pilots to master and accidents did happen including one Swordfish plane that had to make a forced landing into the Irish Sea off Preesall after losing control. The plane was lost, but the crew survived and made it back to shore. Others were not as lucky and the site did suffer some serious accidents, including a crash during a tricky night exercise in 1944, which proved fatal. This was one of many bombing ranges on Morecambe Bay because of its sparse population and location.

Rossall School's Dual Purpose

Located between Cleveleys and Fleetwood on the promenade, Rossall School is a large private school and one of the most significant and oldest sites on the Fylde. Its main use during the war was as accommodation for relocated government departments including the Department for Pensions and the Board of Education. Its large rooms and size were ideal and the space was much needed. Its rifle range was also used by many units in the area, including the Home Guard. With large numbers of training recruits using the site, many coming from RAF Squires Gate, special trams were commissioned as transport to and from the school. In fact, it was so popular that a spur on the tramway was created bringing the trams right to the school (the track is now hidden under newer developments). The school had ammunitions buildings and a small dump. Numerous temporary buildings were erected, which meant that the students had to leave the space. All moved to Naworth Castle in Cumbria to continue their education. The government departments, some of which would later form the Department for Work and Pensions (DWP), eventually moved to permanent sites further inland and the students were able to return. The school also formed a partnership with a London institution – Alleyns School in Dulwich – so the pupils could get away from the Blitz.

One Local's Sea Ordeal

The story of Brian Clarke from Lytham is a remarkable story of survival against the odds. After entering the war as a teenager, he found himself on board the SS *Sithonia*, a British Merchant Navy ship. Working on merchant shipping was one of the most dangerous jobs in the war with the ever present threat of enemy attack from above and below. This proved to be true when whilst sailing to South America the ship was torpedoed by a German U-boat off the Canary Islands, however, Brian managed to board the lifeboat before the ship went down. This was only the beginning of his ordeal as he then spent three weeks drifting around the ocean surviving on a miniscule amount of fresh water. Eventually the boat landed on the West African Coast. Brian was safe at last although he had landed in a French colony run by the Vichy government, who saw Britain as enemies after they destroyed the French Fleet in North Africa. He had to spend six months in detention, albeit lucky to be alive. Brian sadly passed away in 2012 but his memory will live on in Sara Allerton's critically acclaimed novel called *Making Shore*. Brian also gave many speeches about his wartime experiences around the Fylde Coast.

Agriculture on the Fylde

As we know, Britain at war was in desperate need of home-grown goods with large campaigns such as 'dig for victory' being promoted. The area played its part with many people turning to growing vegetables. Larger spaces were turned over to growing food including local golf courses. Marton had its own market gardens and there were more allotments in the town than in most places, which were all utilised often to supplement the rations. Larger scale farming was particularly important on rural Fylde. Today, it's home to some very large farms and it was the same then, the sheer number of small halls and farm buildings you see whilst looking at a map of the area is testament to its thriving agricultural past. The farms often used 'land girls' who helped to feed the nation and the flat Fylde which, along with north of the River Ribble, housed the best of Lancashire's farm and pastureland. There were also large farms around the Wyre and Fleetwood and some Second World War farm machinery (often repairs had to be improvised) and an air-raid siren are on show at Farmer Parr's Animal World in Fleetwood (itself the site of a rogue bomb landing on its field during the war). As well as feeding the country, some food was 'siphoned off' from the local farms and found its way onto the local black market. I would guess that most farmhouses were not without their Sunday roasts and despite tough regulations, there were well-known ways of bending the rules.

Barton Hall Command Centre

Barton Hall on the A6, north of Preston was requisitioned by the RAF during the war to serve as the headquarters of No. 9 Fighter Group. The group's objective was to provide air defence to the North and parts of the Midlands and Wales. Thus, the headquarters was a very important building for the area protecting against German air attack (which included regular planned attacks on Liverpool, Merseyside, Manchester and Barrow-in-Furness as well one-off incidents). The site was in charge of numerous airfields, including RAF Squires Gate and, probably its busiest field, at Speke on Merseyside. It had to process information from many sources most notably radar and the Observers Corps. The threat would then be mapped and decisions based on the intelligence gathered. The command centre can include nearly forty confirmed German 'scalps' among its successes.

Staining at War

The village of Staining was chosen as a site to send some of Britain's 'undesirables'. The British Government decided that 'travellers' would not be able to conform with restrictions placed during the war and viewed them with suspicion (if not with open hostility). It was decided that the village's Thornfield holiday camp would be used to house the groups. The site situated in the heart of the village near to The Plough Inn kept the groups under supervision. It was not a particularly nice thing to happen in the village and not many people are aware that the site now used for fun and leisure had a chequered past. As well as the camp, Staining Mill was used as an observation post as the site had good views towards Poulton and Blackpool, as well as towards the railway line and rural Fylde, proving useful as a vantage point for local Home Guard units.

A German Exhibition

In 1943, a captured German plane was displayed at the market in the centre of Blackpool. The plane, which was a Messerschmitt 109 fighter plane, proved a popular attraction with locals and holidaymakers alike. As well as the propaganda benefits, it was hoped the plane would help to raise money for the war effort. Blackpool managed to raise the grand sum of £1,800,000 during the 'Wings for Victory' week alone.

ICI at War

The large ICI chemical plant on the banks of the River Wyre near to Thornton worked for the war effort as well. The huge site, which had its own railway connection and sidings onto the Fleetwood to Poulton line, created a number of chemicals for the war. Some of the synthetic materials were of critical importance to certain fields, one example being a chemical produced at the site, which was very important for developing clear photographs to be interpreted by Allied command. The site, which has closed recently, had a long history of production and the large chimney used to be a landmark that could be seen for miles. The area was vast (having its own power station), specialist (many manmade discoveries in the fields of plastic/polymers can be attributed) and shrouded in secrecy during the war with workers forced to adhere to strict confidentiality rules at the time.

The site was chosen by ICI because of its proximity to the Preesall salt mines and brine was pumped across the River Wyre site to be processed via a pipeline. The site needed the salt to produce chlorine, which was used extensively in new products. Chlorine has many uses in cleaning but the gas can be turned into a chemical weapon and was used as such in the trenches of the First World War (and reportedly smells like pineapple). Clandestine work was going on under government direction at the site with new projects being undertaken.

Many people worked at the site with varying degrees of security clearance. A regular ferry brought people into site from Wardleys Creek (a small port that has operated since Tudor times) on the opposite side of the river. As victors of the war, Britain publicly displayed the stored German gas after the invasion before dumping it in the Baltic Sea but we too produced large quantities of chemical weapons during the conflict, it was just lucky for everyone that none were used.

The Thornton site was deemed important enough to defend and monitor which suggests that something of high strategic importance was taking place there. An anti-aircraft installation was reportedly built on Central Drive near to the site which was also an approach area for the nearby docks. Due to the size of the site a small fleet used the area and one ship, *The Calcium*, sank on a regular voyage to North Wales. The vessel hit a mine *en route* and sank with one crew member, a fireman on the ship, losing his life. The company's sister ship, *The Sodium*, managed to rescue the other crew members and stop further loss of life. Many of the ship's crew members were decorated for the various acts of bravery and comradeship.

RAF Plane Down

An RAF fighter was forced to make an emergency landing on Blackpool beach. The incident, which happened in 1940, attracted an excited crowd. The plane soon became stuck and the incoming tide threatened the rescue attempt. With the brute force of many men with ropes and the help of the Blackpool lifeboat crew, the aircraft was saved.

Accidently Unearthing the Past

In 2011, construction staff working on a development for the Sandcastle Water Park unearthed an unusual hole in the promenade. It unexpectedly revealed a sizeable brick-room complex. Many different hypotheses surrounded its purpose, ranging from the sensible to the bizarre. After consulting old maps, it was eventually determined to be an old air-raid shelter. The discovery generated a fair bit of local interest, especially since initially the council could not explain its purpose. With over 2,000 air-raid shelters built in the resort it comes as no real surprise that this particular one had been forgotten about. Shelters were produced very

Crowds enjoying a Blackpool holiday and a well-earned break from austerity.

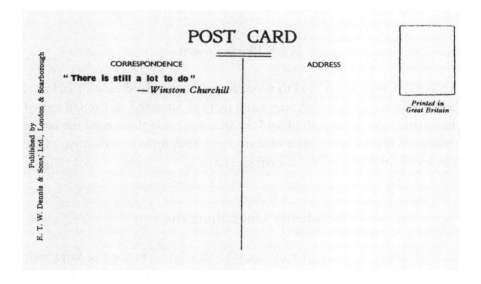

Winston Churchill utilises unusual methods to spread propaganda messages on the reverse of the above postcard.

quickly and in large numbers, and proper planning was not always necessary or possible. An old photograph proved that the promenade structure was a shelter and it is likely that there are more undiscovered sites around the area in unexpected places.

Pilling Sea Defences

Perhaps the most formidable fortified location lay on the quiet Over Wyre coast-line near to the small village of Pilling. The defence was built into the existing sea wall and served a dual purpose, to protect the skies over the port of Fleetwood and to protect the vulnerable quiet coastline from unwanted landings. The defence lay on the coast near to the sands off Pilling Lane and near to the historic Fluke Hall. The defence had space for five large guns in an anti-aircraft role. The site was extensive and the position was protected by pillboxes and barbed wire. Normally manned by local Home Guard units, it looked out over the quiet sea. It was an important geographical position in one of the only unpopulated parts of the Fylde coastline. The geographical features of extensive sands, marshland and calm sea meant it was a particularly vulnerable part of the country and could have been used for an Axis landing (particularly as a secondary site after a larger landing further south) and therefore had to be protected. In front of the site, there were significant anti-glider defences to stop airborne landings on the sands. The site was also near to important ports in Fleetwood (it protected the eastern approaches to the port) and the smaller port of Sunderland Point (famous for its grave of a slave child) together with the more significant Glasson Docks complex (over the sea at the Lune estuary and part of a larger defence of Glasson, which included manned roadblocks). From a command viewpoint, it was an ideal site for an anti-aircraft role in the defence of the north west coast. Thanks to the way the war turned, the site proved largely unnecessary and guns were not placed there permanently.

Air Crash at Fleetwood Beach

In 1945, a large Wellington bomber crash-landed slightly out to sea near Fleetwood beach, and five of seven crew members lost their lives. Servicemen and locals tried to rescue and recover the men by moving heavy parts but most died on impact. The plane landed upside down. There were other registered crash sites around the Lancashire coast as the air traffic in the area was significant thanks to the large number of busy airfields dotted around.

Weapons on Display

Captured German fighters were not the only prized 'scalps' on display for the locals and tourists alike. Towards the end of the war, one of Blackpool's piers was to exhibit a display of fearsome German weaponry. Central Pier had a V1 and V2 rocket on display. The same weapons had been causing havoc in the capital and the south east of the country and they were of great interest to the public. Such attacks even made it as far as Lancashire (after overshooting their original target on the east coast) although they did not make it as far west as the Fylde. A photograph shows that they were housed in makeshift buildings situated on the pier with the public being charged an entry fee. A photograph also shows a replica German U-boat tower on display on the same pier.

Protecting the Fylde's Water Supplies

One of the great secret fears was disruption of clean water supplies as a result of enemy bombing. Numerous overground water tanks were constructed including many along Blackpool's promenade to ensure continuity of supply. The threat, particularly before the war, was taken extremely seriously as cracking reservoirs and disrupting water transportation would have been disastrous for this essential service. The Fylde Coast was particularly vulnerable as the water supply came mainly from Stocks reservoir in the Trough of Bowland along pipes covering a substantial distance. The reservoir was only a few years old at the time of the war and was built (flooding an entire village in the process) to provide water mainly for the growing population of the area as existing reservoirs around Grizedale were no longer adequate. Archived documents show that the Germans had mapped pipelines around Manchester including the pipes of the Fylde water board in the Trough of Bowland.

It is clear that water sources in the area and the country as a whole were heavily protected, as can be seen by the location of pillboxes. For example, there are numerous dotted around the canals (places like Nateby, Cabus, etc.) between Preston and Lancaster, indeed some Fylde water board pipes cross over the canal via bridges. This was to protect the vital watercourses in the county. Many reservoirs such as Rivington, built to supply Merseyside/Wigan, Longdendale, built to supply Manchester, and Denton/Audenshaw, servicing areas for water arriving from Derbyshire, have pillboxes for this very reason. Water had to be preserved as well as protected and wasting water was deemed irresponsible; baths were to be shallow and taps turned off properly. It was hard for gardeners as sprinklers and hoses were not to permitted. Blackpool had a big tradition of market gardening, and large swathes of Marton (where many new-build houses were subsequently built) were under glasshouse and water restrictions were a problem for many locals. Some gardening books from that time have a note from the Fylde water board reminding locals that sprinklers should not be used.

Trams at War

Like many operations in Blackpool during the war, the tram system and its workers had to make do and improvise. Running a large fleet was not an easy task in such conditions and the company did well to maintain the service for the duration. With many of the normal workers being conscripted into the military, the jobs once again fell to the women. Staff shortages in 1940 meant the corporation took the decision to bring women into the tram service for the first time. Initially around 400 women worked mainly as conductors and ticket 'clippies', although by the end of the war women worked in every aspect of the service from mechanics to drivers. Without this added labour, the service would have ceased. The war operated as a great liberator and traditional stereotypes were put aside. In many cases, the hard work done during the war was rewarded afterwards as a legacy of fairness continued into the future. The war certainly sped up the move towards equality and no one could argue with what women achieved in places previously deemed as male preserves.

As well as dealing with staff shortages, the trams were busier than before the war. With large numbers of troops, tourists and civil servants flocking to the resort, the trams felt the strain. They often had poor equipment and novice drivers and were full to the brim. In 1943 over 75 million journeys were made on the Fylde's tram system. Queues were common and tempers flared. Civil servants that had been relocated to the resort felt that they should be given preferential treatment over the tourists – on one occasion workers finished their shift at the Norbreck Hydro and then staged a sit-down protest on the track. Around forty trams were eventually held up and the tense situation had to be diffused by a sizeable police operation. It is worth noting that the tram network was more extensive then than it is now, with routes running up Talbot Road to Layton and a Marton loop and a track running up Lytham Road to the tram sheds near the airport.

The vehicles that operated the many routes had to be stored, maintained and serviced in a time when space was at a premium. Large parts of the shed systems had been turned over to the war effort. Rigby Road was used to train wireless operatives and the storage sheds were used as a NAAFI site.

The depot was ringed by high security fences and protected by sentry guards as an important military site. Marton tram sheds were completely taken over, first by the RAF (as a technical training school), and later as a satellite site for Vickers (producing wings), and the corporation lost housing space for fifty trams. There were grumblings between the military and tram personnel as they often got in each other's way but no major clashes were reported. Other shed depots took over the tram storage burden such as Bispham and Fleetwood (on Corpse Road) where redundant rolling stock was stripped and scrapped. To make matters worse the trams had to be adapted for the war. They were painted green during the conflict as a shortage of cleaners meant dirt showed up against the traditional cream, lights in the cabs were blackened to adhere to the blackout rules and steps were taken to stop trolley wires sparking as it was feared evening trams would attract unwanted overhead attention.

Some expansion took place with a siding being built at Rossall School for special trams that were put on to ferry servicemen to the practice range at the school. The trams often held up traffic to and from Fleetwood, and thus it was decided to build a spare track to stop the obstruction. There were plans put together to run a track all the way up to Common Edge Road to serve the busy Vickers factory, although they did not materialise. At the end of the war the 'Bandwagon' tram, which had been painted during the war with military scenes to raise money for various campaigns, was draped in Allied flags and toured the town. This brought an end to a unique chapter in the life of the town's famous tram network.

CHAPTER 23

FORTIFIED WARTIME DEFENCE POSITIONS

Blackpool and the Fylde's fortified defence positions fall into two main categories: to protect against a coastal invasion, called the 'Coastal Crust', and to protect areas of strategic importance, such as airfields. Creeping into the boundary there is also a strategic defensive line around the A6 called the 'Western Command Stop Line No. 15'.

Coastal Crust defences were spread right along the coast of Britain to deter and hamper German invasion attempts. The majority were built around 1940–41, some hastily as the Battle of Britain took place overhead and there was a real threat of German invasion. As you would expect from a coastal area such as the Fylde Coast there was and still is evidence of a significant number of fortified positions mostly set in concrete to protect strategic points facing seaward to thwart sea bound invasion activity. This was common around the British Isles but is, of course, unique to coastal areas.

Many of the defences in the area were used to defend airfields and command posts. For example, there are a number of positions protecting RAF Squires Gate. These areas would be important in the event of an invasion and there was a real threat of parachute attacks, hit and run raids, and general sabotage. A good example of the need to protect strategic points during an invasion can be seen in the Pacific Island clearing operations undertaken by the US army and navy against entrenched Japanese defenders in which the ability to hold an airfield could make or break a position.

Anti-aircraft base on the sand dunes.

The third type of position was a defensive or strategic line. There were a number of these lines around the country to protect against German advancement. These tended to be second lines of defence and in most cases were critical to the country. The line we see inland towards the Trough of Bowland would have come into effect if the Coastal Crust defences were breached at Blackpool and, in essence, Blackpool had fallen. The defence lines inland would have still been of use to Blackpool as they may have held the troops back and given the defence time to strike a counter attack or force them back to the beaches or to a tactical withdrawal/surrender. Should an invasion of the Fylde Coast have taken place, ignoring the Government's call for 'keep calm and carry on' (one of the slogan's intentions was to reduce large civilian movements, which could hamper the British ability to mount an effective counter measure) much of the Fylde population may have retreated beyond this defence line. Defence lines were seen as hugely important and protected specific highly prized positions and, in our case, the point of the defence lines was to protect communication lines between the north and south. If you think of the A6, the railway and some positions further north in areas such as the Shap Fells where several important communication lines exist in a narrow geographical area, had the Germans crossed this line they may have been able to cut British communications on the west coast to areas further north and in Scotland. The taking of the west coast mainline, which runs through the area, would have hampered the ability to move troops and supplies. The loss of such lines may have left certain areas in a position where surrender would have been inevitable. It is best to think of military strategy as a large game of chess, with every move giving a positive or negative externality over a decisive victory.

There are also occasions when different types of defensive positions meet each other and the best example of this is near to Blackpool and the Fylde Coast around Glasson Dock, at the mouth of the River Lune near Lancaster, in which Coastal Crust positions meet the defence line. There is also a possible strategic defence of a port as well, all within a few miles. This is one reason why this area was highly defended with a number of pillboxes and even a road block.

Intact pillbox on Common Edge Road, initially built to protect the airfield.

There are numerous types of fortified defensive positions. The most common type of defence used in the area were pillboxes, which were normally made from reinforced concrete that would have provided some protection for gunners. Other types include gun emplacements, coastal gun emplacements and anti-tank contraptions. The location of these sites almost certainly would have influenced defensive and operational decisions made by the local commanders. For instance, the Home Guard would work around these positions. How fortified and important a position was would determine who was left to defend it, e.g. regular soldiers or reserves.

It may seem strange that there are a substantial number of fortified positions in the area, with the Fylde Coast being out of the way of the south where invasion was likely. The fact is the Lancashire coast was seen as vulnerable to an invasion and quiet areas such as Pilling Sands and Morecambe Bay were ideal to land troops. The threat to the west coast and Lancashire came from the Germans using Ireland as a base for a sea and airborne invasion. In this case, far from being out of the way it would have been in the thick of it. It turned out that the invasion did not happen and the Germans favoured an invasion of the south coast, codenamed 'Operation Sealion', but this intelligence was obviously unknown at the time. Ireland was not entirely neutral due to old rivalries dating back to the Easter Rising and Irish Independence, and the country had many German spies. The IRA planned to placate the population in order to allow Germans access to the country should they require it and thus there was a threat to the west coast which needed to be addressed, this goes to explaining why the area was still heavily defended (albeit not on a scale seen in places such as Brighton and Eastbourne).

Below is a list of all the registered defensive positions in the area, stating what sort of defence, details of the position and so on, with an introduction to some of the local context about the sites. Most of this information came from a very good scheme that sent volunteers out to map all the local Second World War positions in Britain and give details about the site. These were then uploaded to a centralised database, in this case via the 'Archaeological Data Service', which has links to many types of historic places. In essence, a small part of a huge conservation of knowledge regarding the Second World War that needs to be preserved.

N.B. All locations are according to the Archaeology Data Service.

Type of structure	pillbox (variant)
Location ID	s006483
Composition	clay, brick & concrete
Construction	1940–41
Condition	good, some graffiti
Location	on railway bridge over Devonshire Road, near existing Burtons Factory, North Shore, Blackpool

Which position did it belong to? Lancashire Coastal Crust defence

Additional Information

The location suggests it may have protected strategic roads in the area with Talbot Road and Devonshire Road nearby, hampering inland advancement. It could have also been used to protect trains entering or leaving North Station, which was considerably larger than its present day size, particularly trains leaving the station and heading towards Preston in a hurry. The pillbox can be clearly seen when passing under the bridge. It also has a number of shooting holes. It is worth remembering that the road has since been lowered to allow cars to pass safely under the railway line.

Type of structure	pillbox
Location ID	s0013099
Composition	reinforced concrete
Constructed	1940–41
Condition	bad, with damage, very overgrown
Location	in a small wood within existing boundaries of Blackpool airport, off Leach Lane, St-Anne's-On-Sea opposite Leach Lodge Farm

Which position did it belong to? RAF Squires Gate defence

Additional Information

Leach Lodge Farm, which is over 400 years old, sits very close to the centre of the main runway of Blackpool airport, and near the auxiliary runway, which are both used today. The idea of these pillboxes was to provide the ability to direct a wide range of fire towards the airstrips. Airfields were seen as hugely vulnerable from air attack involving enemy paratroopers. The pillboxes situated at airports were not normally designed to protect against heavy fire but lightly equipped parachute soldiers. They were normally placed to offer protection to the runways and provide a range of fire to exposed areas. The location, on the St-Anne's-On-Sea side of the airport, is also the closest to public access and houses and to the main runway, it would therefore have been an ideal point of entry for the enemy in the event of an invasion at sea and for sabotage and fifth columnists generally.

Type of structure	pillbox
Location ID	S0013227
Made from	reinforced concrete
Date constructed	1940–41
Condition	fair
Location	close to Plumpton village, near Blackpool

Which position did it belong to? Lancashire Coastal Crust defence

Additional Information

The location is set just off Preston New Road, Blackpool, past the Whitehills roundabout, which would suggest protection of a main road out of Blackpool (this was before the M55 motorway was built). The position, however, given via the grid reference on the Archaeology Data Service, puts it set off the road in farmland just at a farm track entrance to Penny Farm (which is now home to the World Horse Welfare charity). The author does not know whether there was an important site at the farm or not, the pillbox is also near to some important electricity pylons and transfer stations that it could have been protecting.

Type of structure	pillbox
Location ID	s00132096
Composition	clay, brick and reinforced concrete
Construction	1940–41
Condition	fair, covered in some graffiti
Location	inside Blackpool Airport at west end of Division Lane

Which position did it belong to? RAF Squires Gate

Additional Information

Situated inland to the rear of the airport, it would have probably been there to protect the start of the main runway, which starts adjacent to the western end of Division Lane.

Type of structure	pillbox
Location ID	s0013220
Composition	reinforced concrete
Constructed	1940–41
Condition	good
Location	inside boundary of South Shore cricket ground at the junction of Division Lane and Common Edge Road, Blackpool

Which position did it belong to? RAF Squires Gate

Additional Information

Protecting a large, open field type entrance to the perimeter to the rear of the airport, near to the previous pillbox. It also protected Common Edge Road, which the enemy may have used to try and flank the airport to attack from both sides. It is visible from Common Edge Road on the airport side (west) just after passing the traffic lights near to the Shovels pub, at the corner of the cricket club close to the road. It is situated next to the Queensway Road in the corner of the field. It is often used to display advertising banners, and one can clearly see inside the box.

Type of structure	pillbox variant
Location ID	S0013095
Composition	clay, brick with reinforced concrete
Constructed	1940–41
Condition	good
Location	junction of Leach Lane and Blackpool Road, St-Anne's-on-Sea, within boundary of airport

Which position did it belong to? RAF Squires Gate

Additional Information

The position is similar to the Leach Lane farm position listed above, but is slightly further southward. It protected the approach to the other pillbox together with the dirt track entrance and also against an assault around the flat land (now part of the St Anne's Old Links golf course) at the side of the airfield. It would have offered a good range of fire to the exposed grass area at the back of the airport.

Type of structure	pillbox variant
Location ID	S0013097
Composition	reinforced concrete and steel
Constructed	1940–41
Condition	good
Location	in small wood (Salisbury Gardens) near access road to Stanley Park aerodrome (Woodside Drive now Blackpool zoo)

Which position did it belong to? it is officially listed as Lancashire coastal defence on the Archaeology Data Service website, however it is protecting Stanley Park aerodrome and not the coast, although the fate of one is linked to the other

Additional Information

This was in place to protect the road entrance to Stanley Park aerodrome, which was where Vickers bombers were assembled. It is in a strategic position protecting the entrance road to the aerodrome, which would have led to East Park Drive. The box has a model of a Home Guard soldier standing on top and has a plaque presented by the Blackpool Civic Trust. It has also been used to promote a talk about the conflict to children studying at local primary schools as part of an educational programme.

Type of structure	pillbox
Location ID	s00123234
Composition	reinforced concrete
Constructed	1940–41
Condition	removed
Location	it was located, using the grid reference given on the Archaeology Data Service website, on the outer edge of the Blackpool De Vere Herons Reach (now De Vere Village Hotel) golf course near to Lawson's field and the paths leading to Marton Mere
Which position did it belong to?	it is officially listed as Lancashire coastal defence on the Archaeology Data Service website, however it is protecting Stanley Park aerodrome and not the coast, although the fate of one is linked to the other.

Additional Information

The position would have been on the outer edge of the aerodrome as the main hangars, which are still used by the zoo for the elephants, are located at the other side of the hotel. It would have protected the edge of the aerodrome and looked over the open expanses of the airfield and possibly Marton Mere and Lawson's field. One can assume that its removal was a result of the development of the golf course belonging to the hotel. There used to be a rubbish dump on the site of the golf course, which stopped more buildings being built there possibly due to the presence of methane gas. The rubbish dump also meant that frogs kept invading one of the bars if the door was left open, providing great amusement for the drinkers. The pillbox may have been demolished as part of the landfill site development.

Type of structure	five gun emplacements
Location ID	not available
Composition	concrete
Constructed	1940–41
Condition	fair, they were bricked up in summer 1986, the tops are only visible as the bottom of the structures were hidden during improvements to the sea wall
Location	Pilling Village, near Blackpool, part of the sea wall near Fluke Hall

Which position did it belong to? Lancashire Coastal Crust defences

Additional Information

The five gunning placements would have looked out over Morecambe Bay towards Cockerham. I suspect they were there to protect a landing from the shore against the exposed marshes (you can see them if you travel on the road from Pilling to Galgate) and would have served effectively in protecting the small bay where the sea encroaches inland over that part of rural Wyre. It is also the first part of coastline uninhabited on the Fylde Coast (except the sand dunes at St-Anne's-on-Sea). The sea defence was built to house guns, although most of the time it was unarmed. The site had a Home Guard office and huge amounts of protective barbed wire. The site also relied on newly built communications telephone exchanges, perhaps purpose-built in 1937, in the nearby village of Pilling. There were also unmanned anti-aircraft guns perhaps protecting the port of Fleetwood and, to a lesser extent, the approaches to Glasson Dock. Anti-glider defences were also placed in front of the emplacements for approximately 1,000 yards into the marsh. Allied commanders often feared superior German gliders (developed when the Treaty of Versailles banned powered German aircraft production). This is one of the most substantial defensive positions on the Fylde Coast.

Type of structure	anti-landing obstacle
Location ID	not available
Composition	concrete and iron
Constructed	1940–41
Condition	dug up and on its side
Location	Freckleton marsh, near Grange Farm
Which position did it belong to?	Lancashire Coastal Crust defences

Additional Information

It consisted of an iron and concrete base, which was buried and had two vertical lengths of railway line sticking up. This was either to protect the marsh area against enemy landing (it was significant as it was next to Warton aerodrome) or to hamper a landing via the Ribble (which was still navigable at the time).

Type of structure	coastal battery gun site
Location ID	not available
Composition	concrete
Constructed	1940–41
Condition	built into sea wall
Location	Fleetwood, in front of the model yacht pool
Which position did it belong to?	Lancashire Coastal Crust defences

Additional Information

Built into the sea wall, it would have protected against enemy ships trying to mount a sea base landing further inland. It is a very good position and would have in essence cut the bay off (any ships would have been destroyed trying to pass). It would have also served to protect the mouth of the River Wyre and the inland port.

Type of structure	gun emplacement
Location ID	not available
Composition	concrete base with walls
Constructed	1940–41
Condition	very bad
Location	in front of Fairhaven Road/ Lightburn Road, St-Anne's-on-Sea, and adjacent car park

Which position did it belong to? Lancashire Coastal Crust defence

Additional Information

It is now used as a children's play pit and was part of a number of defences around the south end of St Anne's beach. It is possible that there was a command post there and this would explain the concentration of defensive positions. The lake also sticks out into the sea and would have been a vulnerable landing position in its own right.

Type of structure	coast battery
Location ID	not available
Composition	clay brick
Constructed	1940–41
Condition	very bad
Location	Fairhaven Lake

Which position did it belong to? Lancashire Coastal Crust defence

Additional Information

This would have housed a large gun pointing out to sea and protecting against ships moving up and down the Fylde Coast. The wall of the structure is now used to form part of the ornamental rockery wall at Fairhaven Lake.

Type of structure	coastal gun battery site
Location ID	not available
Composition	concrete
Constructed	1940–41
Condition	good
Location	Outer Promenade, Fleetwood, near model yacht pool

Which position did it belong to? Lancashire Coastal Crust defence

Additional Information

This would have worked with the battery nearby in order to protect against possible enemy landings.

Type of structure	pillbox
Location ID	soo13098
Composition	reinforced concrete
Constructed	1940–41
Condition	good, some graffiti
Location	in small wood east of the A585 road on south side of junction, B5409 Rossall Lane and B5268 Fleetwood Road South, near Fleetwood.

Which position did it belong to? Lancashire Coastal Crust defence

Additional Information

This is located in the middle of the peninsular between the River Wyre and the coast, near the Nautical College and it is likely it would have been there to protect the thin strip of land, which is vulnerable as it is surrounded by water. It would also have protected the approaches to Fleetwood from the south. This area was important as it could have been used to cut off the Fleetwood isthmus and indeed was the only way in and out of the port via land.

Type of structure	pillbox
Location ID	s0013232
Composition	reinforced concrete
Constructed	1940–41
Condition	fair
Location	Newton-with-Scales

Which position did it belong to? Lancashire coastal defence

Additional Information

It is located on the main Blackpool Road before the approach to Lea town. It lies in a small wood, at the inland side of a stream leading to the Ribble and is possibly a form of defensive line to protect a crossing (waterways and canals were often protected as important navigation routes). The second possibility is that it served to protect a war site as there was a POW and searchlight site (later closed as it was not needed) in the area. The author does not have the coordinates for the exact location of the site, but it was supposed to be near a wood and this is the most likely.

Type of structure	pillbox type fw3124
Location ID	5006929
Composition	reinforced concrete
Constructed	1940–41
Condition	good, the base is exposed
Location	Westby-with-Plumpton near Peel Hall Bridge

Which position did it belong to? Lancashire Coastal Crust defences

Additional Information

The pillbox served the main route inland out of Blackpool (the modern day Preston New Road) in the times before the M55. It would have been the best way to advance inland from a coastal landing, thus a major artery that needed defending. It is a 'type 24' pillbox, which has large embrasures and the box faces the road offering a good range of fire to approaching vehicles from Blackpool.

Type of structure	row of anti-tank pimples, or 'dragon's teeth'
Location ID	not available
Composition	concrete
Constructed	1940–41
Condition	good/overgrown
Location	running parallel to the South Fylde railway line for approximately 6m, near to Sandringham Road in Ansdell
Which position did it belong to?	Lancashire Coastal Crust defences

Additional Information

These obstacles were built near to the Royal Lytham golf club. The golf club like others in the area had defences of its own. In this case, an anti-tank ditch was dug across the golf course. There were also other similar defences in the area, some of which were removed as part of the preparation of the course for the 1988 British Open Golf Championships.

Type of structure	anti-tank block
Location ID	not available
Composition	concrete
Constructed	1940–41
Condition	fair
Location	Brock, near to Billsborrow
Which position did it belong to?	Western Command Stop Line No. 15

Additional Information

A range of concrete anti-tank blocks placed along the main road in the area built to hamper any tank movements along the artery.

Type of structure	pillbox
Location ID	SD 495 474
Composition	reinforced concrete
Constructed	1940–41
Condition	fair
Location	Cabus
Which position did it belong to?	Western Command Stop Line No. 15

Additional Information
Part of a series of pillboxes protecting the line built near to the A6 road.

Type of structure	anti-tank ditch
Location ID	not available
Composition	earthwork
Constructed	1940–41
Condition	good
Location	south-east of Inskip
Which position did it belong to?	defence of HMS Nightjar airfield

Additional Information
An existing agricultural ditch was widened and deepened to stop any enemy tanks attacking the airfield.

Type of structure	gun emplacement
Location ID	not available
Composition	reinforced concrete
Constructed	1940–41
Condition	good
Location	east of Inskip
Which position did it belong to?	defence of HMS Nightjar airfield

Additional Information
The main embrasure faces west. It is situated in a field next to a drainage ditch.

Type of structure	gun emplacement
Location ID	not available
Composition	reinforced concrete
Constructed	1940–41
Condition	filled with earth up to the roof in order to support a JCB digger involved in clearing a drainage ditch
Location	north-east of Inskip
Which position did it belong to?	defence of HMS Nightjar airfield

Additional Information
Situated at the convergence of three large agricultural drainage ditches.

This book does not cover Garstang as it lies on the east side of the A6, but there were a large number of important defences as part of the stop line. These included a gun emplacement at Fowlers Hill and a defensive cylinder protecting part of the River Wyre. There is a fortified concrete cube located near to Nateby Hall on the west side of the Lancaster Canal, which during the war was a goods artery serving the important docks at Preston.

Some defences not included in the above are listed on the following page (these were mainly anti-aircraft gun positions with some parts surviving):

Norbreck

There was a manned anti-aircraft position located on the seafront near to the Norbreck Hydro Hotel, which protected the skies over the town centre. The site also used the nearby church hall of St Stephens on the Cliff as a base for the people who operated the site.

Sand dunes

There was a large anti-aircraft gunning position located on the edges of RAF Squires Gate. The site is the seaward side of the railway line and is situated in the Lytham St Anne's Nature Reserve on the inland side of Clifton Drive. The site has a large 'H' shaped concrete base, which would have formed a support for the gunning position. On the base there is what appears to be some writing that says 'RIP Pte [private] Booth 1944' and was, perhaps, written by a member of the Armed Forces manning the position about a friend lost during the war. At the side of the track and behind the modern green fence, there is also an unusual looking stone-clad concrete building. It is not used for anything now and looks old and it may have been part of the position, but there does not appear to be much information available about the structure. There is also a large metal grid near to the site, which led underground. It looks out of place although it is probably a later addition to the area.

South Shore

There are references on a couple of different websites about an anti-aircraft gunning position being located between Lytham Road and St Anne's Road, near to where the modern day car park is (more railway sidings in the war days). The site is likely to have protected the other side of the town centre, to the Norbreck position and was allegedly fitted with the latest radar defences.

Lytham

Two anti-aircraft guns were placed next to where the Blackpool and the Fylde college buildings stand as part of a greater defence of the Fylde Coast.

Thornton

There are a couple of references online to an anti-aircraft gunning position located on Central Drive in the village. It is possible that it formed part of a defence of the approach to Fleetwood Port (there were defences also at the seafront in the town and Over Wyre at Pilling) as well as the important, if potentially clandestine, wartime operation at ICI.

These positions were largely unnecessary and would not have seen action all of the time. Enemy aircraft did visit the area on semi-regular occasions but manpower, shells and effectiveness were limited. The successes of the guns did improve later on as the technique and technology got better, but certainly, for the early war years they would have served more of a reassuring presence than anything. Huge concrete blocks were placed along the golden mile facing out to the sea. These served as a visible reminder of the dangers that being positioned on the coast could bring in the event of an enemy attack.

Such was the speed in which such defences were installed that many were never properly recorded, but the author has listed those that he is aware of. As well as sizeable sites there were many smaller wartime structures throughout the area. The author grew up in the Watson Road area of the town near to the park and there were numerous sites around. For instance, the attractive grass verge on Windermere Road once had an air-raid shelter on it, a photo of which survives. There was also a garage on Coniston Road, which had been fortified with cement (although this possibly was down to the perceived threat of the Cold War). The author remembers there being a shelter still surviving around the back of the Arnold School (now Arnold KEQMS School) playing fields. The old Blackpool South Station, situated at the end of Station Road near to the bridge and the old scrap yard, had been adapted for use during air raids. This just goes to highlight the sheer number of things all round Blackpool, which existed during the conflict and can be found in many other areas as a legacy of the Second World War.

CHAPTER 24

AFTER
THE WAR

After the war had ended in Europe it left a lasting legacy on the Fylde Coast. Although the loss of life had ceased and people could relax as enemy bombers no longer flew overhead, the effects of the war were everywhere to be seen for many years after the conflict. It could be argued that Britain was the moral winner but economic loser of the war, with many people believing the British were worse off than defeated Germany. Britain had fought tooth and nail and put everything it had into surviving, but the economic consequences of this were disastrous. The country was broke, destroyed and the population had to endure rationing for many years afterwards. America had funded the country and wanted the money back – Britain had no choice other than to pay up. The situation was at its worst immediately after the war ended and before the Marshall Plan was implemented in 1948. The country didn't really fully recover from the war until the 1980s and lost a lot because of the 'finest hour', including the Empire and independence (being overly reliant on America for years to come). Britain became a much quieter voice on the world stage. It was not all in vain though, because as well as victory, the country gained the Welfare State and it could be argued that the notion of Empire needed to be dissolved. The moral courage and pride felt by the nation during the Second World War still survives in many people to this day, without it this book would not have been written.

Rationing continued for years to come as everything was in short supply and even bread rationing (which had been avoided during the years of conflict) eventually came in thanks to a poor wheat crop in 1946. It was not

Blackpool's war memorial taking pride of place on Princess Parade.

until 1954, nearly ten years after the end of the war, that rationing ended completely in Britain. This was particularly hard for many people to stomach as they had won the war, but felt like they were worse off and there were no longer reports of fabled war successes to boost morale and remind them why the sacrifices were necessary. Conditions on the Fylde were not great and, in 1947, some locals decided to leave. They chose South Africa as their destination as it had been on the winning side but had largely avoided the subsequent problems that Britain was facing. Over twenty people decided to make use of a disused large military truck and set off after a farewell party at Blackpool Town Hall in search of a better life in Africa.

Other more pressing issues came to the fore after the war as many people needed to be decommissioned, housed and found work. Everyone had suffered during the war and people wanted a fairer society without the pre-war problems. Again, Blackpool played its role perfectly when arguably the single most important government document of the twentieth century was hammered out in all its detail in the many boarding houses in the town during the war and then implemented by these same workers after the conflict. Many civil servants had chosen to stay in the area and they helped to engineer the Welfare State under the direction of one of the greatest Britons of the time, the social economist William Beveridge. The Welfare State was probably only second to the defeat of fascism as a positive outcome of the war and the town had a unique place in its history. We often take the Welfare State for granted but it was a piece of equality that no government since has yet had the courage to remove and it ensured social provision for the country's most needy via the NHS, the provision of state pensions and employment support and its introduction was accelerated thanks to the wishes of a wartorn public.

This need for change was instigated by the Labour Government being elected to power after the war. The public voted Clement Atlee by a landslide in the 1945 election, the so-called 'Khaki election'. The Labour Party took the critical decision not to enter into another coalition government when in the town's Winter Gardens during the party conference in May of that year and this led to the party's greatest success. The reasons for their victory were chiefly around their pledge of building a better, fairer Britain and the socialist politics of the day scored a bullseye with the voters. Many people, not least observing foreign leaders, were surprised at the result as they thought that Winston Churchill was certain to win. Churchill was still popular and was met with large crowds of supporters wherever he went, but his political ideas did not capture the public's imagination. Everyone was grateful for the way he had run the war and wanted to show support, such as when he was made a Freeman of Blackpool in 1946. He started his journey in Lytham with his wife, surrounded by adoring fans, and he continued down the promenade until he reached the town for a reception to express the gratitude of the locals for his leadership and stance during the conflict. The town wanted to celebrate and remind itself of the 'highs' of the war having won at great cost to the nation. Other less welcome events occurred in 1946 as a direct legacy of the conflict when two large sea mines washed up along the famous beach and another RAF plane crash cost the lives of three just off North Pier.

Implementing social changes took time and, in 1948, nearly 9,000 people were on Blackpool's housing waiting list, many returning soldiers. This need for housing shaped the town into what it is today, and many of the outlying housing estates, which greatly increased the scale of the town, were built to service this need, including Grange Park and Mereside. Jobs were a worry as the war had meant permanent employment for almost everyone, the Vickers factory eventually closed after a stint building prefabricated houses for the cause, bringing with it high unemployment around the area.

In 1948, Field Marshall Montgomery was made Freeman of Blackpool in another grandiose civic ceremony. Tourism was still affected by the shortages, as although small petrol rations were now available to all, it was not until four years after the war that the illuminations shone again. These illuminations were however more appreciated than ever before and quite symbolic as the war had raised the question of whether they would ever shine again. The need for fun in a harsh Britain again meant Blackpool benefited and was full for years to come. With rationing in full force and a steady flow of visitors, it fuelled what became known as the 'great rock racket'. Many local rock factories blatantly ignored the rationing, which was deeply unpopular at the time, and produced the famous confectionery for the willing visitors. The black market was huge and thriving and many rock workers' families didn't go hungry. Organised criminals came in from the big cities bringing illicit goods into their areas, which they then sold at highly inflated prices. It was big business and made many headlines as authorities tried in vain to stop the practice. It did not come to a complete stop until the end of sugar rationing in 1953, when long queues were reported in the resort's sweet shops and factories as people stocked up in celebration.

AFTERWORD

If you were to ask someone when they were most proud to be British, the majority of their answers would revolve around two world wars and one world cup. Winston Churchill frequently tops 'Greatest Britons' polls and history fondly remembers the British attitude during the war. Sometimes, this nostalgia can be somewhat rose-tinted. Military men are often praised but have questionable statuses as heroes, such as Field Marshall Montgomery who was suspected of taking the credit for other people's actions, and Arthur 'Bomber' Harris, whose policy of carpet-bombing civilian areas would probably make him a war criminal in today's terms. Whereas the much-mocked Neville Chamberlain was simply trying his best to bring peace. What is clear is that the war defined the country and laid the foundations for the generally accepting, modern and liberal society which make us what we are today. Britain today is simply great, not without its problems and things I would change, but we are, in my eyes, the greatest country in the world for which we owe a lot to the dark years of the war. The Fylde Coast played a big part in this and I can't think of any other area in the country that played such a pivotal role. The Fylde was an important piece in a critical jigsaw and its success would not have been possible if it were not for the hard work of locals and visitors alike. I hope you have found this an interesting read and that the book serves, if only in a small way, to help this proud history be remembered. I for one look back on Blackpool's role during the war with fondness and I'm proud of the people who worked towards this legacy.

Lightning Source UK Ltd.
Milton Keynes UK
UKOW07f0644181114

241769UK00001B/106/P